The Life of General Robert E. Lee

In Easy Words For Children

Illustrated

Mrs. M. L. Williamson

Copyright 1895

REPRINTED BY

The Scuppernong Press

Wake Forest, NC
www.scuppernongpress.com

The Life of General Robert E. Lee For Children, In Easy Words
By Mrs. Mary L. Williamson

Edited by Frank B. Powell, III

©2022 The Scuppernong Press

First Printing

The Scuppernong Press
PO Box 1724
Wake Forest, NC 27588
www.scuppernongpress.com

Cover and book design by Frank B. Powell, III

All rights reserved

Printed in the United States of America

No part of this book may be reproduced or transmitted in any form or by any means, electronic or mechanical, including photocopying, recording, or by any information and storage and retrieval system, without written permission from the editor and/or publisher.

International Standard Book Number ISBN 978-1-942806-48-6

Library of Congress Control Number: 2022944405

CONTENTS

Chapter   **Page**

Introduction iii

Preface v

The Sword of Robert E. Lee vii

I. Birth and Youth 1

II. A Young Engineer 5

III. A Cavalry Officer 11

IV. A Confederate General 19

V. A Confederate General (*Continued*) 27

VI. A College President 45

VII. A People's Hero 69

General R. E. Lee's Farewell Address to His Soldiers 77

INTRODUCTION

Ever since I was a young boy, Robert E. Lee has been my hero. I read everything I could find about Lee. This book had long been out of print when I came along, but after recently discovering it, we felt the need to republish it for a new generation of young readers.

You will find no one in history who equals Lee. Not just his military career, but his integrity and the way he lived his life. He was a devout Christian in all aspects of his life. We can find example after example of this. No one in history can even come close.

Mrs. Williamson intended for this small book to serve as a supplemental textbook to be used in public schools. Of course, this will not happen in today's Marxist, cancel culture, public/government schools. But, parents can, and should, use this book to teach their children about one of the noblest people in American history.

This edition is reprinted in a modern typeface with small changes to modern punctuation and grammar standards. Most of the original illustrations are included as printed in the 1895 edition.

We hope you enjoy our efforts. Please share this book with your children, grandchildren, nieces and nephews, grand nieces and nephews, cousins and other young people you may know. For if we don't share our history, it will die with us.

— Frank B. Powell, III
Editor

Unveiling of Lee Monument
At Richmond, VA, Friday, May 29, 1890

PREFACE

In preparing the *Life of Lee for Children,* for use in the Public Schools, I beg leave to place before teachers good reasons for employing it as a supplementary reader.

First, I urge the need of interesting our children in history at an early age. From observation I find the minds of children who study history early expand more rapidly than those who are restricted to the limits of stories in readers. While teaching pupils to read, why not fix in their minds the names and deeds of our great men, thereby laying the foundation of historical knowledge and instilling true patriotism into their youthful souls?

Secondly, in looking over the lives of our American heroes we find not one which presents such a picture of moral grandeur as that of Lee. Place this picture before the little ones and you cannot fail to make them look upward to noble ideals.

This little book is intended as auxiliary to third readers. I have used the diacritical marks of Webster, also his syllabication. In compiling this work I referred chiefly to General Fitzhugh Lee's *Life of Lee*, and Reverend J. William Jones' P*ersonal Reminiscences of R. E. Lee.*

Mary L. Williamson

New Market, VA
September 28, 1898

The Sword of Robert Lee

Words by Moina   Music by Armand

Forth from its scabbard, pure and bright,
    Flashed the sword of Lee!
Far in the front of the deadly fight,
High o'er the brave, in the cause of right,
Its stainless sheen, like a beacon light,
    Led us to victory.

Out of its scabbard, where full long
    It slumbered peacefully—
Roused from its rest by the battle-song,
Shielding the feeble, smiting the strong,
Guarding the right, and avenging the wrong—
    Gleamed the sword of Lee!

Forth from its scabbard, high in air,
    Beneath Virginia's sky,
And they who saw it gleaming there,
And knew who bore it, knelt to swear
That where that sword led they would dare
    To follow and to die.

Out of its scabbard! Never hand
    Waved sword from stain as free,
Nor purer sword led braver band,
Nor braver bled for a brighter land,
Nor brighter land had a cause as grand,
    Nor cause a chief like Lee!

Forth from its scabbard! All in vain!
    Forth flashed the sword of Lee!
'Tis shrouded now in its sheath again,
It sleeps the sleep of our noble slain,
Defeated, yet without a stain,
    Proudly and peacefully.

The Life of General Robert E. Lee

CHAPTER I
Birth and Youth

Robert Edward Lee was born at Stratford, Westmoreland County, Virginia, on the 19th of January, 1807.

His father, General Henry Lee, had been a great chief in Washington's army. They sometimes call him "Light-Horse Harry Lee." While with Washington, he was ever in front of the foe, and his troopers were what they always should be — the eyes and ears of the army.

After the war he was Governor of Virginia, and then a member of Congress. It was he who said in a speech made before Congress after the death of Washington, that he was "First in war, first in peace, and first in the hearts of his countrymen." He also said, "Virginia is my country; her will I obey, however sad the fate to which it may subject me."

The long line of Lees may be traced back to Launcelot Lee, of Loudon, in France, who went with William the Conqueror upon his expedition to England; and when Harold had been slain upon the bloody field of Hastings, Launcelot was given by William the Conqueror an estate in Essex. From that time the name of Lee is ever an honorable one in the history of England.

In the time of the first Charles, Richard Lee came to the New World and found a home in Virginia. He was a man of good stature, sound sense, and kind heart. From him the noble stock of Virginia Lees began. He was the great-great-grandfather of Robert, who was much like him in many ways.

Robert's mother was Anne Hill Carter, who came from one of the best families of Virginia. She was a good and noble woman, who lived only to train her children in the right way.

Stratford

Stratford, the house in which Robert was born, is a fine old mansion, built in the shape of the letter H, and stands not far from the banks of the Potomac River and near the birthplace of Washington. Upon the roof were summer houses, where the band played, while the young folks walked in the grounds below, and enjoyed the cool air from the river and the sweet music of the band.

He had two brothers and two sisters. His brothers were named Charles Carter and Sidney Smith, and his sisters Anne and Mildred.

When Robert was but four years of age his father moved to Alexandria, a city not very far from the Stratford House, where he could send his boys to better schools. But he was not able to stay with them and bring them up to manhood. Shortly after he had moved to Alexandria, he was hurt in Baltimore by a mob of bad men, and he was never well again.

When Robert was six years old, his father went to the West Indies for his health. While there he wrote kind letters to his son, Charles Carter Lee, and spoke with much love of all. Once he said, "Tell me of Anne. Has she grown tall? Robert was always good." He wished to know, also, if his sons rode and shot well, saying a Virginian's sons should be taught to ride, shoot, and tell the truth.

When he had been there five years, and only grew worse, he made up his mind to return home. But he grew so ill that he was put ashore on Cumberland Island at the home of a friend. He soon gave up all hope of life. At times his pain was so great that he would drive his servants and every one else out of the room. At length an old woman, who had been Mrs. Greene's best maid, was sent to nurse him. The first thing General Lee did when she came into the room was to hurl his boot at her head.

Without a word, she picked up the boot and threw it back at him. A smile passed over the old chief's face as he saw how brave she was, and from that time to the day of his death none but Mom Sarah could wait on him. Two months after the sick soldier landed he was dead. His body was laid to rest amid the cedars and flowers of the South, and it has never been moved to Virginia.

Mom Sarah

At this time Robert was only eleven years old. If he was a good boy, it was his mother who kept him so, for he never knew a father's care. His mother once said to a friend, "How can I spare Robert! He is both a son and a daughter to me."

About that time the girls and other boys were away from home, and she had no one but Robert to care for her. He took the keys and "kept house" for her when she was sick, and also saw to all of her outdoor work. He would run home from school to ride out with her, so that she might enjoy the fresh air and sunshine. When she would complain of the cold or draughts, he would pull out a great jackknife and stuff the cracks with paper, for the coach was an old one.

So he grew up by her side, a good and noble boy. At first he went to school to a Mr. Leary, who was ever his firm friend. Then he went to the school of Mr. Benjamin H. Hallowell, who always spoke of him as a fine young man.

Robert was fond of hunting, and would sometimes follow the hounds all day. In this way he gained that great strength which was never known to fail him in after life.

The old home, in Alexandria, where his mother had lived, was always a sacred place to him. Years after, one of his friends saw him looking sadly over the fence of the garden where he used to play. "I am looking," he said, "to see if the old snow-ball trees are still here. I should be sorry to miss them."

When he was eighteen years old, he went to West Point to learn to be a soldier. He was there four years, and in that time never got a bad mark or demerit. His clothes always looked neat and clean, and his gun bright. In short, he kept the rules of the school and studied so well that he came out second in his class.

When he came home from West Point, he found his mother's old coachman, Nat, very ill. He took him at once to the South and nursed him with great care. But the spring-time saw the good old slave laid in the grave by the hand of his kind young master.

Uncle Nat

Not very long after, his dear mother grew quite ill. He sat by her bedside day and night, and gave her all her food and medicine with his own hand. But his great care and love could not save her. He was soon bereft of her to whom he used to say he "owed everything."

Some one has said, "Much has been written of what the world owes to 'Mary, the mother of Washington;' but it owes scarcely less to 'Anne, the mother of Lee.'"

Gĕn'-er-al, the head of an army.
Ex'-pe-dĭ'-tion, a voyage; a trip, with an aim in view.
Stăt'-ūre, height.
Drȧughts (drȧfts), currents of air.

Tell what you remember about —
Robert's father.
Robert's mother.
The situation of his home.
Robert's kindness to his mother.
His life at West Point.

CHAPTER II
A Young Engineer

In 1829, when twenty-two years old, Robert entered the Engineer Corps of the United States, and thus became Lieutenant Lee.

It is the duty of these engineers in time of peace, to plan forts, to change the course of rivers which make sand-banks at wrong places, and to do other work of the same kind. Lieutenant Lee was sent at once to Hampton Roads, in Virginia, to build strong works, not dreaming that in after years it would be his fate to try to pull them down.

Robert E. Lee,
Lieutenant of Engineers

Lieutenant Lee was married on the 30th of June, 1831, to Mary Custis, who was the great-granddaughter of Mrs. Washington, and the only child of George Parke Custis, the adopted son of Washington. She lived at a fine old place on the Virginia bank of the Potomac River, called Arlington. At this time Lieutenant Lee was very handsome in face and tall and erect in figure.

Two years after his marriage he was sent to the city of Washington. This change was pleasant to him, for he was then near the home of his wife.

Arlington

In 1837 he was sent to St. Louis to find means to keep the great Mississippi River in its own bed. It was a hard task, but he at last forced the mighty river into the channel he wished. While at work, some men, who did not know what great things he could do, tried to drive his workmen away, and even brought up cannon. Lee did not mind them, but went on with his work, and soon had the great river to flow in the right place.

From St. Louis he was sent to New York to plan and build new forts to protect that great city. He was now a captain of engineers, and was soon to try the horrors of war.

In 1846, a war broke out between the United States and Mexico. "Engineers are of as much use to an army as sails to ships." They have to make roads and bridges, to plant big guns and draw maps, and guide the men when going to fight.

At first, Captain Lee was sent to join General Wool, in the north of Mexico. Not long before the battle of Buena Vista (Bwā'-nä-vees-tä), General Wool sent Lee to see where Santa Anna, the general of the Mexicans, had placed his army. News had come that he was not far off.

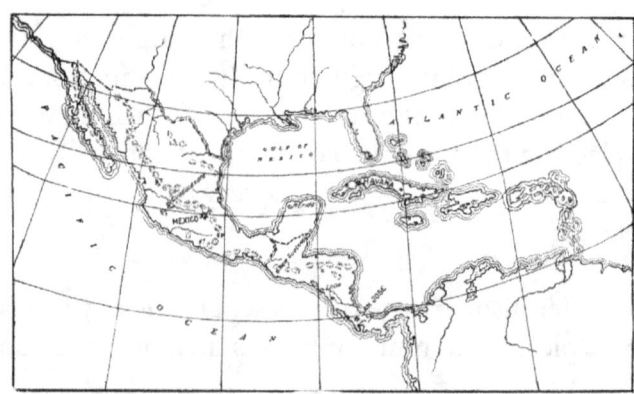

Mexico

6   *The Life of General Robert E. Lee*

Lee rode, with only one man to guide him, into the mountains. After he had been riding for some hours, he saw on a hillside the smoke of fires, and objects which he thought were tents. He went on, in a very cautious way, till he had gotten quite near. Then, he saw the white objects were only flocks of sheep and herds of cattle and mules on the way to market. He found out from the men driving them that Santa Anna had not crossed the mountains, and then went back to his friends, who thought they would never see him again.

Though he had ridden forty miles that night, he rested but three hours before taking a troop of horsemen and going far into the mountains to find out just where Santa Anna had gone with his army.

Soon after this brave deed, Captain Lee was sent to join General Scott in the south of Mexico. He was put to work at Vera Cruz (Vā-rä-krōōs), a large town on the coast. There was a high wall, with strong forts around Vera Cruz. General Scott wished to take this city from the Mexicans. So Captain Lee had to plant big guns and build forts; and to do this he worked night and day.

As they were short of men, he was told to take some sailors from a man-of-war to help with the work. These men began to complain loudly. "They did not enlist to dig dirt, and they did not want to work under a landlubber anyhow." Their captain said to Lee, "The boys don't want any dirt to hide behind; they want to get on the *top*, where they can have a fair fight." Lee quietly showed his orders, and told the old "salt" he meant to carry them out, and pushed on the work 'mid curses both loud and deep.

Just as the work was done, the Mexicans began to fire their guns at that point, and these brave sons of the sea were glad enough to hide behind the "bank of dirt." Not long after, their captain met Captain Lee and said, "I suppose the dirt did save some of my boys. But I knew that we would have no use for dirt-banks on shipboard, that there what we want is a clear deck and an open sea. And the fact is, Captain, I don't like this land fighting anyway; *it ain't clean.*"

Vera Cruz was taken by General Scott in two weeks' time. Then the men went on over hills and vales, till they came to the strong fort on Cerro Gordo. Captain Lee then found a way to lead the Americans to the rear of the Mexicans, who soon broke and fled.

The Life of General Robert E. Lee

While this battle was raging, Captain Lee heard the cries of a little girl, and found by the side of a hut a Mexican drummer boy. His arm had been badly hurt and a large Mexican, who had been shot, had fallen on him. Captain Lee stopped, had the big Mexican thrown off of the boy, and the little fellow moved to a place of safety.

His little sister stood by. Her large black eyes were streaming with tears, her hands were crossed upon her breast, and her hair in one long plait reached to her waist. Her feet and arms were bare. She was very thankful to Captain Lee for saving her brother.

Captain Lee Rescuing Drummer Boy

In a letter to his son from this place, he says: "I thought of you, my dear Custis, on the 18th in the battle, and wondered, when the musket balls and grape were whistling over my head, where I could put you, if with me, to be safe. I was truly thankful you were at school, I hope, learning to be good and wise. You have no idea what a horrible sight a battlefield is."

From Cerro Gordo, they went on fighting battles until they came to the large and rich city of Mexico.

On this march, Captain Lee was always at the front to guide the men. Once, when one part of General Scott's army had lost its way, General Scott sent *seven* engineers to guide it into the right road. They had to cross a huge, rough bed of lava and rock. *Six* of them went back to camp, saying that they could not get across; but, Captain Lee pressed on in the dark, alone and on foot, and brought the men out in safety. General Scott once said it was the greatest feat done by any *one man* during the war

There were many battles fought, but at last the city of Mexico was taken by General Scott. In after years, this great man was heard to say that his great success in Mexico was largely due to the skill and valor of Robert E. Lee, and he was the *best soldier* he ever saw in the field.

In the midst of all this fighting, his boys were ever in his thoughts. This is a part of what he wrote to his son Custis on Christmas Eve, 1846:

"I hope good Santa Claus will fill my Rob's stocking tonight; that Mildred's, Agnes's, and Anna's may break down with good things. I do not know what he may have for you and Mary, but if he leaves you one-half of what I wish, you will want for nothing. I think if I had one of you on each side of me, riding on ponies, I would be quite happy."

Not long after, he wrote to his boys thus:

"The ponies here cost from ten to fifty dollars. I have three horses, but *Creole* is my pet. She is a golden dun color, and takes me over all the ditches I have yet met with."

When the war was at last ended, in 1848, Captain Lee went home for a short rest, after which he was sent to West Point, as the Superintendent of the Academy from whose walls he had gone forth twenty-three years before. His duty was to watch over the studies and training of the boys who would one day be officers in the army.

Corps (kōre), a body of troops.
Of'ficer, one who has charge of soldiers.
Lävä, melted matter flowing from a volcano.
Fēat, a great deed.
Lieuten'ant (lutĕn'ant), an officer next below a captain.

Tell me —
When Robert became Lieutenant Lee.
Whom he married.
Where he was sent in 1837.
What war broke out in 1846.
About a great feat performed by Captain Lee.
Where he was sent in 1848.

The Life of General Robert E. Lee

CHAPTER III
A Cavalry Officer

After being three years at West Point, Captain Lee was sent to Texas as Lieutenant Colonel (kûrnel) of the Second Regiment of Cavalry. Cavalrymen are soldiers who fight on horseback and who carry sabers, and pistols, and short guns, called carbines.

Colonel Lee did not wish to leave the Engineer Corps, as he had become very fond of the work, and had won a high rank in it; but, as he had been promoted to a higher place, he thought it best to take it. When at West Point, he had been a fine horseman. He was still fond of horses and liked to see them fed and well taken care of. Though now forty-six years of age, he still had a firm seat in the saddle and rode well. His regiment was sent to the new State of Texas, where his duty was to watch the Indians and keep them from killing the whites.

Lee chasing the Indians

I have no doubt Colonel Lee enjoyed riding over the vast plains of Texas, but life in the forts was not very pleasant to such a man as Lee. The forts were in the midst of dreary plains, and there were only a few men at each post. The scouting parties were led by lieutenants, and the higher officers would remain at the forts to see that all went right. Such a lonely life did not suit our hero, but he made the best of it.

Near his first post, Camp Cooper, was an Indian Reserve, where the Indians would come to be fed by the Government. When it was cold and food was scarce, they would come in; but when the grass grew in the spring and the game was fat, they would go off and become wild and savage enough to kill those who had been kind to them.

Catumseh, a Comanche chief, was at the Reserve when Lee was at Camp Cooper. Lee thought it would be better to visit him and tell him that he would trust him as a friend so long as he behaved; but if he did not behave he would take him for a foe. Catumseh was not much pleased with Lee's speech, but gave an ugly grunt and said, as he had *six* wives, he was a "big Indian." Lee had better "get *more wives* before he talked." This visit did not do much good. Catumseh was no doubt taking the measure of Lee's scalp, while Lee was displeased with the sly and filthy Indian.

The Comanche Indians were then the fiercest tribe in that region. They ate raw meat, slept on the ground, and were great thieves and murderers. They were fine horsemen, and moved swiftly from place to place on their ponies.

In June, 1856, Lee was sent with four companies of his regiment on an expedition against the Comanches, but they could not be found. The wily Indians had fled to their desert retreats, where foot of pale face had never trod.

From Camp Cooper he writes to Mrs. Lee:

"My Fourth-of-July was spent after a march of thirty miles in one of the branches of the Bra'zos, under my blanket, which rested on four sticks driven in the ground, as a sun-shade. The sun was fiery hot, the air like a furnace, and the water salt; still my love for my country was as great, my faith in her future as true, as they would have been under better circumstances."

The change of weather in Texas is sometimes very great.

In another letter, he tells his wife about a cold wind or norther. "I came here in a cold norther, and though I pitched my tent in the most sheltered place I could find, I found this morning, when getting up, my bucket of water, which was close by my bed, so hard frozen that I had to break the ice before I could pour the water into the basin."

While Colonel Lee rode with his troopers from fort to fort, a dreadful disease broke out among them. Many died, but Colonel Lee did not catch the disease, though he lived among his men and ran great risks. In these sad times, his thoughts were ever with his dear ones at home.

In a letter dated Camp Cooper, June 9, 1857, he tells about the sickness of the troopers:

"The great heat has made much sickness among the men. The children, too, have suffered. A bright little boy died from it a few days since. He was the only child, and his parents were much grieved at his loss * * *. For the first time in my life, I read the service of our Church over the grave to a large number of soldiers." A few days after, he again read the service over a little boy who had died with the disease.

In a long letter from Fort Brown, Texas, December, 1856, he says:

"I thought of you and wished to be with you." He wrote again: "Though absent, my heart will be in the midst of you; I can do nothing but love and pray for you all. My daily walks are alone, up and down the banks of the river, and my chief pleasure comes from my own thoughts, and from the sight of the flowers and animals I meet with here."

In the midst of this wild, lonely life he was ever true to his faith in Christ, which he had professed after the Mexican war.

There was at Arlington a large yellow cat, called Tom Tita. All the family were fond of him, and Colonel Lee among the rest. This led him to write home about the cats he saw in his travels. He told once of a cat called by his mistress Jim Nooks. He was a great pet, but at last died from eating too much. He had coffee and cream for breakfast, pound cake for lunch, turtle and oysters for dinner, buttered toast and Mexican rats, taken raw, for supper. He was very handsome, but his "beauty could not save him." The kindness of his mistress was his ruin.

Tom Tita

Again he told his little girl about a cat which was dressed up. He had two holes bored in each ear, and in each wore bows of pink and blue ribbon. He was snow-white and wore a gold chain on his neck. His tail and feet were tipped with black, and his eyes of green were truly cat-like.

In the summer of 1857, he was made Colonel (kûr'nel) of his regiment. The next fall his father-in-law, Mr. Custis, died, and Colonel Lee went home for a short time. Mr. Custis left Arlington and the rest of his land to Mrs. Lee, and he also willed that at the end of five years all of his slaves should be set free. He had chosen Colonel Lee to see that his will was carried out.

Colonel Lee stayed as long as he could with his lonely wife, and then went back to his post in Texas. It must have been far from easy for him to go back to the wild, hard life on the plains. There were then no railroads. The United States mail was carried on mules, by armed soldiers who rode in a gallop from place to place. Often they were slain by the Indians, who would scalp them and leave their bodies to be found by the troopers as they chased the savages back to their retreats.

Two years more were spent in Texas, when, in October, 1859, we find him again at home, and taking part in a great tragedy.

A man, named John Brown, made a plan to set free the negro slaves who were then in the South, and to kill all the whites. This plot did not succeed, and John Brown and his men took refuge in the Round House at Harper's Ferry. Colonel Lee, who was then at home on a furlough, was ordered to take a band of soldiers and capture these bold men. He went at once to Harper's Ferry and quickly took them prisoners. They were then tried and hung for treason.

Just here, I must tell you that the slaves were blacks, or negroes, who had first been brought to this country from Africa, in 1619, by the Dutch, and sold to the Virginia planters. At first, the planters bought them out of pity, as they were badly treated by the Dutch. But after a time it was found the negroes worked well in the corn and tobacco fields, and they made money for their masters.

Many men at the North were sea-going men, and they soon found out that, by sailing over the ocean to Africa and catching the blacks, they could sell them at a great profit to themselves. This they did, and men both at the North and South bought them, though, even then, there were some people at the South who thought it wrong to buy and sell human beings.

In the State of Georgia it was for a time against the law to hold negro slaves.

After a while, it was found the climate at the North was too cold for the negro to thrive. It did not pay the men at the North to keep them, and so they were sold to the Southern planters.

In the South, the climate was hot, like that of their native Africa, so they did well in that sunny land.

In 1808, it was made unlawful to bring any more slaves from Africa to the United States. The people at the South were glad the trade in slaves was stopped, but the Northern traders were, of course, sorry they could make no more money in that way.

When the negroes were first brought from Africa, they were uneducated but, after a few years, they learned the speech and customs of the whites; and, more than all, the worship of the true God.

There were now four million negroes in the South. There was great love between the blacks and their masters, as we have seen when John Brown tried to get the former to rise up and slay the whites. For years, there had been a feeling in the North that it was wrong to own slaves, and some of the people began to hate the South and to try to crush it.

Colonel Robert E. Lee at John Brown's Fort, Harper's Ferry

The South felt they owned the slaves under the law, or Constitution of the United States, and that they ought to be let alone. They also claimed the slaves, as a class, were better treated than any other working people in the world. They, moreover, said the Southern States had a perfect right to go out of the Union, if they wished, and set up a government for themselves. This the North denied; and thus they quarreled about the rights of States, and slavery, and other things, until they began to think of war.

In a short time after the John Brown Raid, Colonel Lee was back at his post in Texas, but he was much troubled at the state of his dear country. He loved the Union and had lived nearly all his life in its service; but he knew that Virginia was in the right, and that he could not fight against his native State.

So, when the war came, he left the United States Army to fight for Virginia and the South.

He was offered the chief command of the United States Army if he would remain in the "Union" service. He knew if he went with the South he would lose his rank, and also his lovely home — Arlington, but "'none of these things moved him;' his only wish was *to know, that he might walk the path of duty.*"

He said to Mr. Blair, who came to offer him the command of the army: "If I owned the four millions of slaves in the South, I would give them all up to save the Union, but how can I draw my sword upon Virginia, my native State?" So, when Mr. Lincoln called for troops to send against the South, Lee turned his back upon "wealth, rank, and all that a great power could give him, and offered his stainless sword to his native State." His great soul was wrung with grief, but he obeyed the call of duty.

He went at once to Richmond, and was made Major General of the Virginia troops. His three sons also joined the Confederate army.

General Lee was now fifty-four years old. He had been thirty-two years in the service of the United States.

The great War Between the States ("Civil War") now began. The eleven Southern States which had left the "Union" were now called "The Confederate States of America;" Mr. Jefferson Davis was made president of them, and Richmond in Virginia was made the capital city.

Sā'bers, swords with broad blades.
Furlough (fûr'lō), a leave of absence.
Trea'son (trē'zon), the act of being false to one's country.
Promō'ted, raised to a higher rank.
Rĕg'iment, a body of troops under a colonel.
Trăg'ĕdy, an action in which the life of a person is taken.

Virginia State Capitol, formerly occupied by the Confederate Congress

The Life of General Robert E. Lee

What do you know about —
Cavalrymen?
Colonel Lee's life in Texas?
Catumseh?
The Comanche Indians?
The negroes?
John Brown?
The wish of Lee?
What he deemed his duty?
The great War Between the States ("Civil War")?

CHAPTER IV
A Confederate General

In this little book I cannot tell all that happened during the War, but only as much as will relate to our hero, General Lee.

There were now two governments — one at the North; the other at the South. Mr. Abraham Lincoln was President of the North, or Federals, while Mr. Jefferson Davis was the President of the South, or Confederates. The first thought of the North was to defend Washington, their capital city; while the South was just as busy taking care of Richmond, and getting arms and troops ready for war.

In this war, brother fought against brother, and friend against friend. It was a time of great trouble all over the land. At the North, one hundred thousand men were enlisted in three days. At the South, the feeling was more intense. Men rushed to arms from all parts of the country.

You must notice that from the first of the war, the South was much poorer in the number of men and arms than the North. There were at the North eighteen millions of whites; while at the South, there were only six millions. Through all the South, there could be found only fifteen thousand new rifles and about one hundred thousand old muskets.

The Federals wore a uniform of blue, while the Confederates were clad in gray; hence they were sometimes called "the blue" and "the gray."

The first blood which flowed in this war was shed in Baltimore. The Sixth Massachusetts Regiment, as it was passing through the city on its way south, was attacked by a band of men who loved the South and could not bear to see them marching on to fight their brethren. In the fierce street fight which followed, several men were killed. This happened on April the 19th, 1861.

The first gun of the war was fired at half-past four o'clock April 12, 1861, at Fort Sumter, in South Carolina. This fort was taken by the Confederates after a fight of thirty-four hours, in which no one was hurt on either side.

General Robert E. Lee in West Virginia

During the first months of the war, General Lee was kept in Richmond to send Virginia men, who came to fight for the South, to the places where they were most needed. All around Richmond were camps, where men were trained for war. The largest of these camps was called "Camp Lee," after our hero. But in July, 1861, Lee was sent to Western Virginia, and was, for the first time, commander of troops in the field.

Just then, there were heavy rains and a great deal of sickness among the men of his small army, so that he was not able to attack the enemy, as he had planned.

After some time, it was thought best to give up Western Virginia, and General Lee went back to Richmond, where he stayed only a short time. In November, 1861, he was sent south to build a line of forts along the coasts of South Carolina and Georgia. In four months' time he did much to show his skill as an engineer.

But a large Northern army, under General McClellan, was at the gates of Richmond, and Lee was sent for to take charge of all the armies of the South. Very soon, a battle was fought at Seven Pines, May 31st, which stopped General McClellan's "On to Richmond." In that battle General Johnston, the commanding general, was badly wounded, and General Lee was put in his place. Lee was swift to plan and as swift to act. His task was hard. The hosts of the North were at the gates of Richmond. The folks on the house-tops could see their campfires and hear the roar of their cannon. Lee at once began to make earthworks, and to place his men for battle. Every day, now, a fine-looking man, clad in a neat gray uniform, might be seen riding along the line.

He wished to know what was going on in the camp of the foe, and now the right man came forward. His name was J. E. B. Stuart, best known as Jeb Stuart. He led his brave troopers quite around the army of the North and found out all that Lee wished to know. He was ever after this, until his death, the "eyes and ears" of Lee.

"Stonewall" Jackson now came from the Valley with his brave men, and Lee at once began the "Seven Days' Battle." Stuart was "the eyes and ears" of Lee, and Jackson was his "right arm," as you will learn before you get through with this little book.

For seven days the battle went on, and at last the Army of the Potomac, under General McClellan, was forced back to the James River, and Richmond was saved from the foe by the skill of Lee and the valor of his men.

Lee now marched north towards Washington City, and in August, 1862, met the army of General Pope and fought the Second Battle of Manassas. Lee had made a bold plan to put the army of Pope to flight. He sent Stonewall Jackson fifty-six miles around to the rear of Pope, while he (Lee) kept him in check in front. Jackson's men marched so fast that they were called "foot cavalry." They ate apples and green corn as they marched along, for they had no time to stop. Only one man among them knew where they were going. Little cared they, for Stonewall Jackson led the way.

On the evening of the second day, Jackson, with twenty thousand men, was between Pope and Washington city. Lee was in front of Pope with the rest of the army.

General Jackson fell upon Manassas Junction and took three hundred prisoners and many carloads of food and clothes. After the men had eaten what food they wanted, they burned the rest and moved away.

Jackson found a good position from which to fight, and when Pope's men came up was ready for them. They fought all day, and when the powder and shot gave out the Southern men fought with stones.

The Life of General Robert E. Lee

All this time Lee, with most of the men, was coming round to help Jackson. How eagerly Jackson looked for help! He had only twenty thousand men against three times that many. At last Lee came up, and the battle was won (August 30th). Many brave men were killed on both sides, but Lee was the victor. In three months' time he had driven the foe from Richmond, and was now in front of Washington with his army.

He now sent General Jackson to Harper's Ferry, where he took as prisoners twelve thousand men of the North, September 15th. Jackson then hurried back to Lee, who had crossed the Potomac and gone over into Maryland, on September 5, 1862.

Last Meeting of Lee and Jackson

At Sharpsburg sometimes called Antietam (Ante'tam), he again met the fresh army of McClellan and fought one of the most bloody battles of the war. Lee had only half as many men as McClellan, but when, after the battle, Lee thought it best to return to Virginia, McClellan did not follow him. Lee led his army back to Virginia without the loss of a gun or a wagon, and they rested near Winchester, Virginia.

General Lee, in his tent near Winchester, heard of the death of his daughter Annie. She had been his dearest child, and his grief at her death was great; but he wrote thus to Mrs. Lee:

"But God in this, as in all things, has mingled mercy with the blow by selecting the one best prepared to go. May you join me in saying 'His will be done!'"

It was now McClellan's turn to attack Lee, but he was slow to move — so slow that Mr. Lincoln sent him word "to cross the Potomac and give battle to the foe, and drive him south." But still he did not move, and Lee, who was also wanting to move, sent Jeb Stuart over into Maryland to find out what McClellan was doing. That gallant man again went around the whole Northern army, and came back safe to Lee, having found out what Lee wished to know.

The Northern army now came back to Virginia and Lee moved to Fredericksburg, a town on the Rappahannock river.

Burnside was now put at the head of the Northern army in the place of General McClellan, whom Mr. Lincoln accused of being too slow.

Lee placed his men on the heights above the river, on the south side, while Burnside's hosts were on Stafford Heights and the plains below.

At daylight on December 13, 1862, the battle began, and was fought bravely by both sides. But Burnside's men had little chance, since Lee's men from above poured the shot and shell so fast that they could not move forward.

The noise of this battle was terrible, as there were three hundred cannon roaring at once.

Lee at Fredericksburg

Cooke, a great writer, tells us that as Burnside's guns were fired directly at the town, the houses were soon on fire and a dense cloud of smoke hung over its roofs and steeples. Soon the red flames leaped up high above the smoke and the people were driven from their homes. Hundreds of women and children were seen wandering along the frozen roads, not knowing where to go.

General Lee stood upon a ridge which is now called "Lee's Hill," and watched this painful scene. For a long time he stood silent, and then, in his deep, grave voice, said these words, which were the most bitter that he was ever known to utter: "These people delight to destroy the weak, and those who can make no defense; it just suits them."

When the day was done, Lee was again victor.

In less than *six months* Lee had fought *four* great battles — all victorious to his arms, except that of Sharpsburg, which was neither a victory nor defeat. The Southern army was now full of hope and courage. At the battle of Fredericksburg, Lee had only sixty thousand men, while Burnside's army numbered over one hundred thousand. In this battle Lee lost five thousand men, while twelve thousand of Burnside's men lay stark and cold upon the bloody field.

Lee grieved over the loss of his brave men, and for the good people of Fredericksburg who had lost their homes by fire during the fight. He now waited day after day for Burnside to attack, but in vain. At length Lee went into winter quarters in a tent at the edge of an old pine field near Fredericksburg, and began to get ready for fight when the spring came. It was at this time that among a number of fowls given to Lee, was a fine hen which began the egg business before her head came off, and Bryan, Lee's servant, saved her for the egg which he found each day in the General's tent. Lee would leave the door of the tent open for the hen to go in and out. She roosted and rode in the wagon, and was an eyewitness of the battle of Chancellorsville. She was also at the battle of Gettysburg; but when orders were given to fall back, the hen could not be found. At last, they saw her perched on top of the wagon, ready to go back to her native State.

General Lee's Hen

In 1864, when food began to get scarce and Bryan was in sore need for something nice for guests, he killed the good old hen unknown to her master. At dinner, General Lee thought it a very fine fowl, not dreaming that Bryan had killed his pet.

It was now time for Lee to carry out the will of old Mr. Custis and set free his slaves. Many of them had been carried off by the Northern men, but now he wrote out the deed and set them free by law. He wrote thus of

The Life of General Robert E. Lee

them to Mrs. Lee:

"They are all entitled to their freedom, and I wish them to have it. Those that have been carried away I hope are free and happy."

Lee had proved so great a leader that the people of the South began to look to him with great love and hope.

During these battles, of which I have told you, one-half of the Southern men were in rags, and many were without shoes. Yet shoeless, hatless, ragged and starving, they followed Lee and fought his battles. Their pet name for him was "Marse Robert." They knew their great chief cared for them, and would not send them into danger if he could help it; and it was no fault of his if their food was scant and poor. They learned to love and trust him. "Marse Robert says so," was their battle cry.

    Prĕs'ident, the head of a free people.
    Mĕr'cy, kindness.
    Găl'lant, brave; daring in fight.
    Vĭc'tor, one who wins.
    Posĭ'tion, place.

    Tell about —
    The two governments.
    The first blood shed.
    The first gun fired.
    "Camp Lee."
    Where General Lee was first sent.
    The "On to Richmond."
    Jeb Stuart. "Stonewall" Jackson.
    The Second Battle of Manassas.
    Sharpsburg. Fredericksburg.
    The will of Mr. Custis.
    The soldiers' love for Lee.

CHAPTER V
A Confederate General
(*Continued*)

When the spring of 1863 came, the two armies were still in sight of each other near Fredericksburg. A new man, General Hooker, sometimes called "Fighting Joe," had been put at the head of the army of the North. Take note that he was the fourth general that President Lincoln had sent forth within a year to conquer Lee.

Lee watched his new foe, and when he had found out his plans was ready for him. He fell back to a place called Chancellorsville, and there, in the midst of a dense forest, the fight took place (May 2, 3).

While the battle was going on, Lee sent Jackson to the rear to cut Hooker off from a ford in the river. Jackson's men moved through the forest so swiftly and with so little noise that they fell upon Hooker's men with a loud yell before he knew they were near. They rushed out like a thunder-bolt and swept down upon the line like a flash of lightning. The foe did not wait, but turned and fled.

It was now nearly dark, and, as Jackson rode forward to view the way, he was shot by his own men, who, in the dim light, thought he and his aids were a squad of Northern cavalry. He was shot in three places — in his right hand, his left forearm, and again in the same limb near the shoulder. He was placed in a litter and taken from the field. All care was taken of this great and good man, but he died the next Sunday. His last words were:

"Order A. P. Hill to prepare for action. Pass the infantry to the front. Tell Major Hawkes"— he stopped and then said, as if the fight was over, "Let us pass over the river and rest under the trees."

Thus passed away the great Stonewall Jackson, the "right arm of Lee."

For two days after Jackson was wounded, the fight went on and raged with great fury. General Hooker was struck by a piece of wood split off by a cannon ball, and for a time was thought dead.

Lee made bold plans and his brave men carried them out. Stuart, who had taken Stonewall Jackson's command, led his men to battle, singing "Old Joe Hooker, won't you come out of the wilderness."

At last the battle of Chancellorsville was won and Hooker was forced back to his old camp at Fredericksburg.

Chancellorsville was Lee's greatest battle, but its glory was clouded by Jackson's death. General Lee wrote to his wife, May 11, 1863:

"You will see we have to mourn the loss of the good and great Jackson. * * * I know not how to replace him, but God's will be done."

In this battle Lee had only fifty-three thousand men, one-third as many men as Hooker.

General Stonewall Jackson

In June, 1863, Lee again crossed the Potomac and met an army under General Meade at Gettysburg, in Pennsylvania.

Lee had two reasons for this move. One was to get food for his men and horses; and the other to draw the Northern army away from its strong forts around Washington city. He gave strict orders to his men not to steal and rob. This is a part of his order:

"The commanding general thinks that no greater disgrace could befall the army, and through it our whole people, than to commit outrages on the innocent and defenseless. * * * It must be remembered that we make war only upon *armed men.*"

This order, with its noble Christ-like spirit, will remain the "undying glory of Lee;" for all his property had been taken by the Federals. His wife and daughters were homeless, yet he did not fail to return good for evil.

When Lee started into Maryland, he sent Jeb Stuart on ahead to guard the right flank of his army. By some mishap, he crossed the Potomac too far to the east, and soon found the whole Federal army was between him and General Lee. By hard fighting and riding he at last joined Lee at Gettysburg, but not until after the fight had begun. Lee was thus without his "eyes and ears," as we have called General Stuart, and could not tell just where the foe was. Neither Lee nor Meade had planned to fight at Gettysburg, but they fell upon each other pretty much like two men groping in the dark.

For the first two days (July 1, 2) Lee's men drove back the enemy. On the third day, at 1 o'clock P. M., Lee began to fight with one hundred and fifty big guns. For two hours the air was alive with shells. Then, out of the woods swept the Confederate battle line, over a mile long, under General Pickett. A thrill of wonder ran along the Federal lines as that grand column of fifteen thousand men marched, with ragged clothes, but bright guns and red Battle Flags flying, up the slope of Cemetery Ridge. Down upon them came shot and shell from guns on the heights above and round them.

The line was broken, but on they went. They planted their Confederate Flags on the breastwork; they fought hand to hand and killed men at the cannon with the bayonet; but down from the hill rushed tens of thousands of Federals, and many who were not killed were taken prisoners. Few got back to tell the story. That night the stars looked down upon a field of dead and dying men and also upon a sad general. Lee's orders had not been obeyed, and, for the first time, he had been foiled.

Lee afterwards said to a friend, "Had I had Stonewall Jackson at Gettysburg, I would have won a great victory."

He had made a bold plan to attack early in the day; but it was not done, and thus Meade got time to bring up his troops. Meade did not attack Lee, who rested that night upon the same ground as the night before.

Lee now had but little powder and shot. On the next day, the 4th of July, he started his long trains of wounded and prisoners towards Virginia; and, at the same time, buried his dead. That night, in a storm, the army began its homeward march, and reached the Potomac river to find it too high to cross. Calm and brave, Lee sent his wounded over in boats and got ready for Meade. But Meade was in no mood to attack Lee and came up slowly.

While waiting for the river to fall, Lee heard of the capture of his son General W. H. F. Lee.

On the 13th, Lee's men began to cross the river, and by the next night they were again safe in Virginia.

The men lost at Gettysburg were never replaced, for the South had sent forth all her fighting men and had no more to give.

The rest of the year passed without any great battle. Lee's chief concern was to get food and clothes for his men and to watch Meade, who would not give battle.

About this time the city of Richmond presented to Lee a house. This he kindly but firmly refused to take, and begged that what means the city had to spare might be given to the families of his poor soldiers.

Late in November, General Meade moved towards Lee, who had built strong forts at Mine Run. But Meade found the forts too strong for attack and withdrew during the night.

The next year a new man was sent against Lee — Ulysses S. Grant. Lee had now only sixty-two thousand men to meet Grant, who had *one hundred and twenty-five thousand* men, and a wagon train which reached sixty-five miles.

With this large army, Grant crossed the Rapidan River, and marched on to give Lee battle. Lee did not wait for Grant, but went forward and met his hosts in a place called the Wilderness, which was a vast forest full of underbrush, and with only narrow roads here and there. It was a bad place in which to fight a battle, for no man could see but a few yards around him. Cannon and horsemen were of no use, because they could not move through the tangled bushes.

Grant did not know Lee's men were so near. But when they rushed into these wilds and boldly began the fight he had to give battle. For two days, May 5th and 6th, 1864, two hundred thousand men in blue and gray fought breast to breast in the thickets. Men fell and died unseen, their bodies lost in the bushes and their death-groans drowned in the roar of battle.

In the midst of these horrors, the woods caught on fire and many of the wounded were burnt alive. Lee, however, pressed forward, and when night closed had taken a portion of the Federal breastworks.

During the fight of the 6th, General Lee placed himself at the head of some men from Texas to lead the charge. "Hurrah for Texas!" He cried, and ordered the charge. But the soldiers, anxious for their dear general, shouted, "Lee to rear!" A gray-haired soldier seized his bridle, saying, "General Lee, if you do not go back, we will not go forward!" So General Lee reined back his horse and the brave Texans swept on to victory and death.

On the morning of the 7th, Grant made no motion to attack Lee, but that night marched towards Spotsylvania Court House. Lee at once found out his plans and began a race to reach there first. When the front of Grant's army reached the Court House the next morning, they found Lee's men behind breastworks and ready for the fight. Lee had gotten between Grant and Richmond! That evening the two great armies were again facing each other on the banks of the Po River. Here they threw up breastworks, which may yet be seen.

Lee in Front of His Troops

For twelve days, Grant made many attacks upon Lee's lines. Early on the morning of the 12th his men made an opening in Lee's lines and poured in by thousands. Lee's men ran up quickly and soon a most terrible fight took place. The trenches ran with blood and the space was piled with dead bodies, whose lips were black with powder from biting cartridges.

Though Grant held that position, he could not break through the second line. The little army in gray stood as firm as the mountains.

In the fight of which I have just told you, General Lee again rode in front, with hat off, to lead the charge; but General Gordon dashed up and said:

"These are Virginians and Georgians who have never failed. Go to the rear, General Lee."

Then he said to the men: "Must General Lee lead this charge?"

"No! No!" They cried; "we will drive them back if General Lee will go to the rear."

They rushed off and once more hurled back the Federal troops.

Grant now sent his cavalry general, Sheridan, on a raid near Richmond. A fierce battle was fought at Yellow Tavern, in which the famous Jeb Stuart was wounded so that he died the next day. Alas for Lee! Jackson and Stuart were both gone.

Grant again moved to the rear, and Lee next moved to the North Anna river. While Grant was again trying to flank, Lee got to the old works at Cold Harbor. Grant made an attack at daylight. His troops, sinking into a swamp, were killed by thousands, while Lee lost but few men.

A second assault was ordered, but the men would not move forward. About thirteen thousand of their comrades had been killed in less than half an hour, and they could no longer stand the awful fire.

We are told by General Fitzhugh Lee that Lee's men were hungry and mad. One cracker to a man, with no meat, was a luxury. One poor fellow, who had his cracker shot out of his hand before he could eat it, said: "The next time I'll put my cracker in a safe place down by the breastworks where it won't get wounded, poor thing!"

Lee again stood in Grant's way to Richmond. In the battles from the Wilderness to Cold Harbor, Grant had lost sixty thousand men, while Lee's loss was eighteen thousand.

Just before the battle of Cold Harbor, Grant had looked for Sigel to move up the Valley and fall upon Lee's rear. But Sigel was met at New Market on May 15th by Breckenridge with five thousand troops, among which was a band of cadets from the Virginia Military Institute at Lexington. These boys fought like heroes, fifty of them being killed and wounded. Sigel was sent running back down the Valley, and Breckenridge then marched to the help of Lee.

Grant then, on the night of June 12th, began to move his army south of the James river to march towards Petersburg, a city about twenty-one miles south of Richmond.

The famous General Beauregard (Bo're-gard) was at Petersburg with only about two thousand men, as he had sent the most of his troops to the north side of the James river to the help of Lee.

Against these, on the 15th, General Grant sent eighteen thousand men.

Beauregard held these men in check until Lee sent troops to aid him. Lee then came up with the main army, and Grant, having lost ten thousand men, now began to make trenches and build forts to protect his men, as he was going to lay siege to Petersburg, the key to Richmond.

Lee had to defend both Richmond and Petersburg with lines thirty-five miles long, against Grant's army, which was twice as large as his own. In fact, Grant had all the men he asked for; while Lee's ranks were thin and food was scarce. A fourth of a pound of meat and one pound of flour was all each soldier had for one day.

In this stress, it is said Lee thought it best to give up Richmond and march south to join the army there. I do not know the truth of that statement. At any rate, he did not go, but went to work to make his lines stronger and to get in food for his men. One of his great cares was to keep Grant from getting hold of the railroads which brought food from the South and other parts of the country.

Just here, it will be well to give you some of the war prices at that time. Flour brought, in Confederate money, two hundred and fifty dollars per barrel; meal, fifty dollars; corn, forty; and oats, twenty-five dollars per bushel. Brown sugar cost ten dollars per pound; coffee, twelve dollars; tea, thirty-five dollars; and they were scarce and hard to get. Woolen goods were scarce; calico cost thirty dollars per yard, and lead pencils one dollar a piece. Women wore dresses which were made of cloth spun, woven and dyed by their own hands. Large thorns were used for pins and hairpins, and shoes were made with wooden soles. Hats were made by girls out of wheat straw, plaited into a braid and then sewed into shape.

Those were indeed hard times; but in spite of want and care, the spirits and courage of the Southern people did not flag. All food that could be spared was sent to Richmond, and every one hoped for the best.

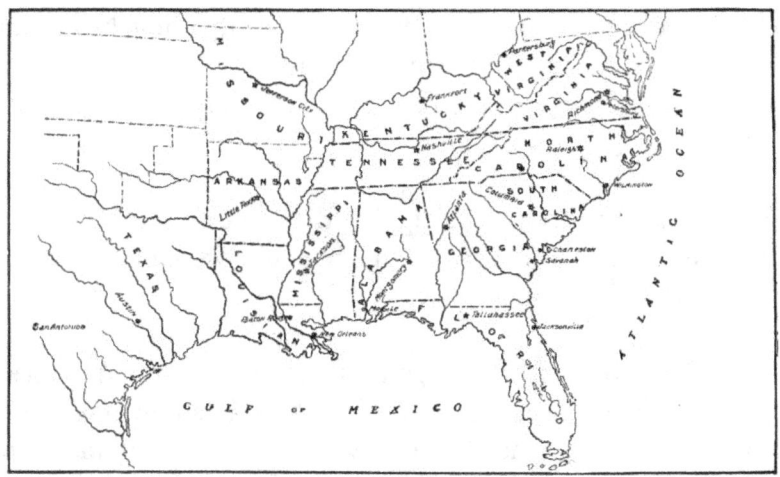

The Southern States

Time after time Grant's men made attacks upon Lee's works, but were always sent back faster than they came, by his watchful men.

The shells from Grant's big guns fell into the city of Petersburg day after day, bursting into the churches and houses, and making the people flee for their lives.

One day, as General Lee was sitting on a chair under a tree at his headquarters, the "Clay House," the balls fell so thick about him that his aids begged him to seek a safer place. He at last mounted his horse and rode away. A moment after, a gay young soldier sat down in the chair and tilted it back, saying, "I'll see if I can fill Lee's place for awhile." Just then a ball struck the front round of the chair and cut it in twain. If Lee had been there, with the chair upon the ground, he would have been badly hurt. All thanked God that he was safe.

On June 22d, the Confederates under General Mahone made a sally from their lines and gave the Federals a great surprise. As the Southern shot and shell burst upon them, they fled back into their lines and the Confederates brought off two thousand prisoners, four cannon and eight flags.

On the same day, there was a fight at Reams' Station, in which the Federals were put to flight and lost twelve guns and one thousand men.

All this time, Grant was making earthworks and forts, and at last carried out a very cruel plan. From a spot out of sight, he had a mine dug until it reached under one of the Confederate forts. In that hole he had caused to be placed a blast of eight thousand pounds of powder. His plan was to blow a hole in Lee's lines and then rush in with a large band of men and take the city.

General Lee found out they were digging the mine and where it was, and had a strong line made in the rear, while big guns were placed so as to fire across the breach when the mine was sprung.

At that time there were only thirteen thousand men in the trenches at Petersburg, as General Lee had been forced to send some of his troops to the north of the James to check a move which Grant had made on purpose to draw off Lee's men from the mine.

Just at dawn, July 30th, the blast was fired. A great roar was heard, and then two hundred and fifty-six men from South Carolina and twenty-two from Petersburg, with guns, large masses of earth, stones and logs, were thrown high into the air. A breach one hundred and thirty-five feet long, ninety feet wide, and thirty feet deep, had been made in the Confederate lines. Those near the spot were at first stunned, and those far away could not think what the noise meant.

Grant's guns fired at once all along the line, and a band of men marched out to rush in through the breach. When they had rushed across the space to the gap, they found a deep pit at their feet.

The Confederates had now gained their wits, and at once opened fire. The storm of shot and shell forced the Federals down into the pit for shelter; but when there, they could not get out. Band after band of Federals were sent forward to charge the works, but they either fell into the Crater or ran back to their own lines.

Two hours had now passed, when black troops were sent to seize the guns which were doing such deadly work. They marched bravely up, but the Confederate fire was too hot for them and they ran for their lives — some into the Crater, and some back to their own lines. White troops were again sent forward, but they, too, were driven back. All this time the Crater was full of wounded, struggling and dying men, upon whom the hot sun beat and shot poured down.

Explosion of The Crater

Soon General Lee rode up, and by his orders, General Mahone, with Weisiger's and Wright's brigades, came up and charged with a yell upon the Federals who had for the first time reached the breastworks. There was a fierce hand-to-hand fight, but the Federals were quickly forced back.

All honor is due to the few men who had so bravely held the breach until help came.

Just at this time a white flag was seen to float above the side of the Crater, which told that some were alive down there and ready to give up.

In this strange fight Grant lost about four *thousand* men and Lee about four *hundred*.

The pluck and skill of Lee and a few men had foiled a well-laid plan and showed what these brave heroes could do after years of toil and battle.

Lee now thought that if he would again send troops to threaten Washington, he might cause Grant to move some of his large army there, and thus give him (Lee) a chance to hurl back the hosts of Grant from Richmond. So he sent General Early down the Valley into Maryland with only ten thousand men.

They went as fast as they could, and on July 9th met, at Monocacy Bridge, General Lew Wallace with seven thousand men. Having whipped him and taken from him two thousand men, Early marched on to Washington.

On the 10th, his troops marched thirty miles, and on the 11th were in front of Washington. But his force was too small and too much worn out to try to attack the city. He coolly camped in front of it all day, and at night after a fight with some Federal troops sent to catch him, went back into Virginia.

This raid of Early's did not move Grant. He left Mr. Lincoln to take care of Washington and kept the most of his men massed in front of Lee's lines.

It was about this time the Federal General Sheridan passed up the Valley and burned two thousand barns filled with wheat and hay, and seventy mills filled with flour. He also drove off and killed four thousand head of stock. The boast was that "if a crow wants to fly down the Valley he must carry his food along."

This was a part of the plan to crush and starve Lee, for a great part of his flour and meat was sent from the Valley.

After many trials, on August 18th Grant at last got hold of the Weldon railroad, which brought supplies from the south. This was a great blow to Lee.

In the fall of this year, when meat was scarce, General Wade Hampton sent a note to General Lee, telling him there was a large drove of beeves in the rear of Grant's army and asked leave to take a force of horsemen and drive out the cattle. General Lee at last told him to go, but urged him to take great care not to be caught.

The men were well on their way when day broke, and rode on until dark, when they came to a halt in a road overhung by the branches of trees. Here they slept, men and horses, till just at dawn they sprang to their saddles, and with the well-known yell dashed into the camp of the foe. The Federals made a good fight for their meat; but at last fell back, and the Confederates captured and drove out more than two thousand beeves. These they brought safe into camp after having two fights and riding one hundred miles. This fresh meat was a great treat to Lee's men and the cause of much fun.

Lee's lines were so close to Grant's at one point that the men would often call over to each other. The Federals called the Confederates Johnny Rebs,

Johnny Reb and Billy Yank

while the Confederate name for the Federals was Billy Yanks. On the day after the beef raid, one of Grant's men called out.

"I say, Johnny Reb, come over. I've got a new blue suit for you."

"Blue suit?" Growled out Johnny.

"Yes," said the other, "take off those greasy butternut clothes. I would, if I were you."

"Never you mind the *grease*, Billy Yank," drawled out the Confederate, "I got that out'n them beeves o' yourn."

Pop! went the Federal's gun, and the Confederate was not slow to pop back at him.

General Lee's life was now full of care; as soon as one attack on his lines was over, another was begun. He lived in a tent and would go down to the trenches himself to see how his men were getting on.

An old soldier relates that one day he came into the trenches when the firing was quite rapid. The men did not dare to cheer, lest they might bring a hotter fire from the foe, but they crowded around him and begged him to go back. But he calmly asked after their health and spoke words of cheer. Then he walked to a big gun and asked the lieutenant to fire, so he might see its range and work. The officer said, with tears in his eyes,

"General, don't order me to fire this gun while you are here. They will open fire over there with all those big guns and you will surely get hurt. Go back out of range and I'll fire all day." General Lee was greatly touched by this, and went back, while the men quickly fired off the huge gun.

Lee needed not only men, but food for those he had. Many men died from cold and want.

The winter of 1864 and '65 was a sad one for Lee and the South. There were no more men in the South to take the place of those who had been killed.

The corn and wheat of the South had been burnt and the cattle killed by the Northern armies. The people sat down to empty tables and had no more food to send their men.

Mrs. Lee, in her sick chair in Richmond, "with large heart and small means" knit socks, which she would send at once to the bare-footed men.

On January 10, 1865, General Lee writes to Mrs. Lee:

"Yesterday three little girls walked into my room, each with a small basket. The eldest had some fresh eggs, the second some pickles, and the third some popcorn, which had grown in her garden. * * They had with them a young maid with a block of soap made by her mother. They were the daughters of a Mrs. Nottingham, a refugee from Northampton county. * * I had not had so nice a visit for a long time. I was able to fill their baskets with apples, and begged them to bring me hereafter nothing but kisses, and to keep the eggs, corn, etc., for themselves."

Lee's men were ragged and starving, but they fought on till April 1st, 1865, when, at Five Forks, the left wing of Grant's large army swept around the right and rear of Lee, and made him give up Richmond and Petersburg.

When the Southern troops were leaving Richmond, by law of Congress the tobacco houses were set on fire to keep them from falling into the hands of the foe. The fire spread, and Mrs. Lee's house was in danger of being burnt. Friends came in and wished to move her to a place of safety, but she was loath to go. The fire had no terror for her as she thought of her husband with his band of ragged, starving men marching with their "faces turned from Richmond." White clouds of dense smoke, with the light of fire in their folds, hung above the city as the Federal army, with waving flags and clashing music, marched in and stacked arms in the Capitol Square.

In the meantime, Lee marched on towards Amelia Courthouse, where he had ordered meat and bread to be sent for his men. But when he got there he found that it had been sent elsewhere, and now real want set in. His men had nothing to eat but corn, which they would parch at night and eat as they marched along. General Lee's plan had been to march south and join General Johnston, but some time had been lost in looking for food, and General Grant's hosts were near at hand.

So Lee fell back towards Lynchburg, but on April 9th, 1865, being entirely surrounded by Grant's vast army, he and his few ragged men surrendered to General Grant at Appomattox Courthouse. Lee had only *eight thousand* men, while Grant's army numbered about *two hundred thousand.*

In all these battles, of which I have told you, General Lee had never been really defeated; but he gave up at last because he had no more men and no more food. The Northern generals had all the men and food they asked for, as they had the world to draw from; but the South, being blockaded, or shut in by Northern ships of war, could not get what she needed from other lands.

Lee did all that courage and genius could do against such odds, and was, without doubt, the greatest commander of his time.

Colonel Venable, an officer on General Lee's staff, tells this story of the surrender: "When I told General Lee that the troops in front were not able to fight their way out, he said 'Then, there is nothing left me but to go and see General Grant, and I would rather *die a thousand deaths.*'"

Another officer says when Lee was thinking of the surrender he exclaimed, "How easily I could get rid of all this and be at rest! I have only to ride along the lines and all will be over. But," he added quickly, "*it is our duty to live,* for what will become of the *women* and *children* of the South if we are not here to support and protect them?"

The Life of General Robert E. Lee

So, with a heart bursting with grief, he once more did his *duty*. He went at once to General Grant and surrendered himself and his few remaining men.

By the terms of the surrender, Lee's men gave up their firearms, but all who had horses took them home, "to work their little farms."

General Grant, it must be said, was most kind to General Lee and his men. He did not ask for General Lee's sword, nor did Lee offer it to him; neither did he require Lee's men to march up to stack their guns between ranks of Federals with flags flying and bands playing. Lee's men simply went to places which were pointed out and stacked their guns. Their officers then signed a parole not to fight again against the *United States*. They were then free to go back to their homes, which, in some cases, were burnt — blight and want being on every side.

After all, Grant did not go to Lee's camp or to Richmond to exult over the men who had so often met him in battle; but he mounted his horse, and, with his staff, rode to Washington. Before going, he sent to Lee twenty-five thousand rations; for, as I have told you, Lee's men had nothing to eat but parched corn.

After the surrender, Lee rode out among his men, who pressed up to him, eager to "touch his person, or even his horse," and tears fell down the powder-stained cheeks of the strong men. Slowly he said:

"Men, we have fought the war together; I have done my best for you; my heart is too full to say more."

Lee Leaving Appomattox Courthouse

"And then in silence, with lifted hat, he rode through the weeping army towards his home in Richmond."

As General Lee rode on towards Richmond he was calm, and his thoughts dwelt much more on the state of the poor people at whose houses he stopped than upon his own bad fortune. When he found all along the road the people were glad to see him and gave him gladly of what they had to eat, he said, "These good people are kind — too kind. They do too much — more than they are able to do — for us."

At a house which he reached just at night, a poor woman gave him a nice bed; but, with a kind shake of the head, he spread his blanket and slept upon the floor.

The next day he stopped at the house of his brother, Charles Carter Lee; but, when night came, left the house and slept in his old black wagon. He could not give up at once the habits of a soldier.

When, at last, the city of Richmond was in sight, he rode ahead with a few of his officers. A sad sight met his view. In the great fire of the 3rd of April, a large part of the city had been burned, and, as he rode up Main street, he saw only masses of black ruins.

As he rode slowly, some of the people saw him, and at once the news flashed through the streets that General Lee had come.

The people ran to greet him, and showed by cheers and the waving of hats and handkerchiefs how much they loved him.

General Lee now went home and there again took up his duty. He had fought for the South, which had failed to gain the victory. He thought it was now the duty of every good man to avoid hate and malice and do all that he could to build up the waste places of his dear land. He had been a soldier for forty years, and, for the first time since manhood, was in private life.

He now enjoyed the company of his wife and children, and as long as he kept his parole and the laws in force where he lived, was thought to be safe. There were, however, steps taken to try him for treason; but General Grant went to the president and told him his honor was pledged for the safety of General Lee, and he wished him to be let alone. So, General Grant's request was granted and no trial took place.

After some months the Lee family left Richmond and went to live at the house of a friend in Powhatan county.

The spring and summer of 1865 was spent by our hero in taking the rest which he so much needed.

Rĕf'ugee', one who leaves home for safety.
Siēge, the act of besetting a fortified place.
Hûrled, thrown.
Gēnius, a great mind.
Surrĕn'der, the act of yielding to another.

What do you remember about —
Chancellorsville?
The death of General Jackson?
Gettysburg?
The Wilderness?
"Lee to the rear?"
Cold Harbor?
The siege of Richmond and Petersburg?
The surrender?
General Grant's kindness?

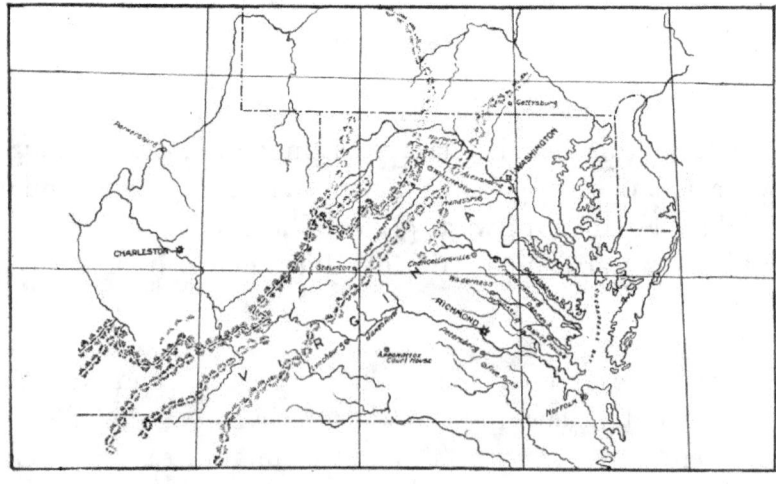

Virginia Battlefields

CHAPTER VI
A College President

In October, 1865, General Lee became president of Washington College, in Lexington, Virginia. Many other places of trust were offered him, but he chose to lead the young men of the South in the paths of peace and learning, as he had so nobly done in times of war.

General Lee rode on his war-horse, Traveler, from Powhatan county to Lexington in four days. As he drew rein in front of the village inn, an old soldier knew him, gave the military salute, and, placing one hand upon the bridle and the other upon the stirrup, stood and waited for him to dismount.

On October 2nd, 1865, General Lee took the oath of office, before William White, Esq., justice of the peace. The General stood, dressed in a plain suit of gray, his arms folded, and his eyes calmly fixed upon Judge Brockenbrough, as he read the oath of office.

The great chief was now changed into a college president. "I have," said he, "a task which I cannot forsake." That task was not easy, for the college had lost much during the war and now had to be built up in every way.

Washington & Lee University and College Chapel

He went to work with great skill and energy, and soon all felt that a great man was leading them.

Some one has aptly said, "Suns seem larger when they set;" so it was with Lee. At this time of his life he appears nobler and grander than ever before. In his quiet study, away from the noise of the world, he gave his time and talents to the young men of his dear South. His earnest wish was to make Washington College a great seat of learning, and for this he worked and made wise plans.

In March, 1866, he went to Washington city to appear as a witness before the committee which was inquiring into the state of things in the South. This was his first visit to any of the cities since the war, and it caused much comment.

General Fitz. Lee tells us the day after his return, he proposed a walk with one of his daughters, who said, in fun, that she did not admire the new hat which he was about to put on. "You do not like my hat?" said he; "why, there were a thousand people in Washington the other day admiring this hat." This was the only time that he spoke of the crowds of people who sought him while in that city.

When his nephew, General Fitz. Lee, wrote to know what he thought of having the Southern dead moved from the field of Gettysburg, he said, "I am not in favor of moving the ashes of the dead unless for a worthy object, and I know of no fitter resting-place for a soldier than the field on which he so nobly laid down his life."

It is sometimes asked if General Lee was content in the quiet of his home at Lexington. This is what he wrote to a friend:

"For my own part, I much enjoy the charms of civil life, and find, too late, that I have wasted the best years of my life."

In his life as College President, duty was, as ever, his watchword. He knew each student by name, and just how well he studied.

Once, when asked how a certain young man was getting along, he said: "He is a very quiet and orderly young man, but *he seems very careful not to injure the health of his father's son*. Now, I do not want our young men to injure their health, but I want them to come as near it as possible."

One of his friends relates that, even amidst this busy life at college, he found time to be the most polite gentleman in town. "How often have I seen him," says this friend, "in the stores and shops of Lexington, talking pleasantly with each newcomer; or, walking a mile through mud and snow to call on some humble family, who will hand it down as an event in their lives that they had a visit from General Lee!"

Seeing, during the first year, that the college chapel was not large enough, he at once began to plan for a new one. He chose the site for it in front of the other houses, so it might be in full view. He then had the plan drawn under his own eye, and did not rest until it was finished and opened for the service of God.

In this chapel his body now rests, as I shall tell you hereafter.

Early in 1870, in the midst of these labors, his health began to fail. There was a flush upon his cheek, and an air of weariness about him which alarmed his friends. Rheumatism of the heart and other parts of the body had set in, and in March, 1870, he went south "to look upon other scenes and enjoy the breezes in the 'land of sun and flowers.'" His daughter Agnes went with him.

On this trip he once more went to see his father's grave, on an island off the coast of Georgia, where, you remember, General Henry Lee was taken when so ill on board ship, and where he died. They placed fresh flowers upon the grave, which they found in good order, though the house had been burnt and the island laid waste.

His health seemed better when again at home; but soon his step was slower, and the flush upon his cheek began to deepen. "A noble life was drawing to a close."

On the morning of October 12, 1870, the news flashed over the wires that General Lee was dead. He had taken cold at a vestry meeting. The church was cold and damp, and a storm was raging outside. He grew chilly, and when he reached home was unable to speak.

Mrs. Lee wrote thus of his last hours:

"My husband came in while we were at tea, and I asked where he had been, as we had waited some time for him. He did not reply, but stood up as if to say grace. No words came from his lips, but with a sad smile he sat down in his chair."

He could not speak! A bed was at once brought to the dining room, and the doctors sent for. At first he grew better, but soon a change came for the worse.

He rarely spoke except when sleeping, and then his thoughts were with his much-loved soldiers on the "dreadful battlefields." Among his last words were, "Tell Hill he must come up."

Once when General Custis Lee said something about his getting well, he shook his head and pointed upward. When his doctor said, to cheer him, "How do you feel today, General?" General Lee said slowly, "I feel better."

The doctor then said: "You must make haste and get well. Traveler has been standing so long in the stable that he needs exercise."

The General made no reply, but shook his head and closed his eyes. Once or twice he put aside his medicine, saying, "It is no use."

On October 10th, about midnight, he was seized with a chill and his pulse became feeble and rapid. The next day he was seen to be sinking. He knew those around him, but was not able to speak. Soon after nine o'clock on the morning of the 12th, he closed his eyes on earthly things and his pure soul took its flight to God.

It was thought that the strain and hardships of war, with sorrow for the "Lost Cause" and the griefs of his friends, had caused his death. Yet, to those who saw his calmness in all the trials of life, it did not seem true that his great soul had been worn away by them.

The college chapel was chosen by Mrs. Lee as a burial place for her husband, and one-and-a-half o'clock P. M. on the 13th of October was the time fixed on for moving the remains to the chapel, where they were to lie in state until Saturday, the 15th of October, the day for the burial.

At the hour named, a long procession, with Professor J. J. White as chief marshal, was formed. Old soldiers formed an escort of honor. Just after the escort came the hearse, preceded by the clergy and twelve pall-bearers. In rear of the hearse, Traveler, the iron-gray warhorse of General Lee, was led by two old soldiers. Then followed a long line of students, cadets and people.

The body was borne to the college chapel and laid in state upon the dais, the people passing slowly by, that each one might look upon the face of the dead. The body was clad in a simple suit of black and lay in a coffin, strewed by loving hands with rare, pale flowers. The chapel was then placed in charge of the guard of honor. This guard of students kept watch by the coffin day and night.

On the 14th, a funeral service was held in the chapel; and on the 15th of October, as I have said, the body was home to the tomb. The flag of Virginia hung at half-mast above the college and a deep gloom rested upon all.

As the procession moved off, the bells of the town began to toll, and the Virginia Military Institute battery fired minute-guns. All was simple and without display. Not a flag was to be seen along the line. The Rev. J. William Jones tells us as follows:

"The old soldiers wore their citizen's dress, with black ribbon in the lapel of their coats; and Traveler, with trappings of mourning on his saddle, was again led by two old soldiers. The Virginia Military Institute was very beautifully draped, and from its turrets hung at half-mast, and draped in mourning, the flags of all the States of the late Southern Confederacy.

"When the procession reached the Institute, it passed the corps of cadets drawn up in line, and a guard of honor presented arms as the hearse went by. When it reached the chapel, where a large throng had gathered, the students and cadets, about six hundred and fifty strong, marched into the left door and aisle past the remains and out by the right aisle and door to their proper place.

"The rest of the line then filed in, the family, with Drs. Barton and Madison, and Colonels W. H. Taylor and C. S. Venable, members of General Lee's staff during the war, were seated just in front of the pulpit, and the clergy and the Faculties of the College and Institute had places on the platform.

"The coffin was again covered with flowers and evergreens.

"Then the Rev. Dr. Pendleton, the dear friend of General Lee, his Chief of Artillery during the war, and his rector the past five years, read the beautiful burial service of the Episcopal Church. There was no sermon, and nothing said besides the simple service, as General Lee had wished.

"When the body had been placed in the vault, the chaplain read the concluding service from the bank on the southern side of the chapel, and then the grand old hymn,

'How firm a foundation, ye saints of the Lord,' was sung by the people.

"The vault is of brick and just reaches the floor of the library. Upon the white marble are these words:

> **Robert Edward Lee**
> **Born January 19, 1807**
> **Died October 12, 1870**

The white marble top has now been replaced by the beautiful recumbent statue by Valentine, a Virginia sculptor.

All the South mourned for Lee. Bells were tolled in cities and villages, and meetings were held to express the grief of the people.

Recumbent Statue of Lee

This is what a little girl wrote to Mrs. Lee:

> "I have heard of General Lee, your husband, and of all his great and noble deeds during the war. I have also heard lately of his death. I have read in the papers that collections are being made for the Lee monument. I have asked my mother to let me send some money that I earned myself. I made some of the money by keeping the door shut last winter, and the rest I made by digging up grass in the garden. I send you all I have. I wish it was more. I am nine now.
>
> "Respectfully,
> "Maggie McIntyre."

Many noble men and women also wrote to Mrs. Lee, and money was given, until now there are two beautiful statues of General Lee — one in Lexington, where he is buried, and the other in Richmond, the city he fought so hard to save.

Virginia mourned for her noble son. The State Legislature passed a bill making January 19th, the birthday of Robert E. Lee, a legal holiday.

On that day, all over the South, meetings are held in memory of him, speeches are made by great men, and children recite poems which honor his name and deeds.

Perhaps no man has ever lived, so great, so good, so unselfish as Lee. Duty was the keynote of his life. In the midst of his greatness he was humble, simple and gentle. He loved little children wherever he met them.

"One day, during the war, a number of little girls were rolling hoops on the sidewalks in Richmond, when General Lee came riding towards them. They stopped playing to gaze at so great a man. To their surprise, he threw his rein to his courier, dismounted, and kissed every one of them. Then mounting, he rode away, with a sunny smile of childhood in his heart and plans of great battles in his mind."

"While in Petersburg, in the winter of 1864, he went to preaching one day at a crowded church, and saw a little girl, dressed in faded garments, standing just inside the door and looking for a seat. 'Come with me, my little lady,' said the great soldier, 'and you shall sit by me.' Thus the great chief and poor child sat side by side."

Once when riding in the mountains with one of his daughters, they came upon a group of children who ran at the sight of him. General Lee called them back and asked:

"Why are you running away? Are you afraid of me?"

"Oh! no, sir; but we are not dressed nice enough to see you."

"Why, who do you think I am?"

"You are General Lee. We know you by your picture."

So great was the love of the people for Lee that, after the war, almost every home had some picture of the great chief.

General Lee knew all the children in Lexington whom he met in his walks and rides, and it was charming to see their joy when he would meet them.

Once, when calling upon the widow of General A. P. Hill, her little girl met him at the door and held out her puppy which she had named after our hero. "O, General Lee," she cried, "here is 'Bobby Lee'; do kiss him." The great man made believe to kiss him and the child was delighted.

In one of the Sunday schools of Lexington a prize was offered to the child who should bring in the most pupils.

A little boy of five went for his friend, General Lee, to get him to go to his school. When told that General Lee went to another school, he said with a deep sigh, "I am very sorry. I wish he could go to our school, and be my new scholar."

General Lee thought it quite funny, and said kindly;

"Ah! C_____, we must all try to be *good Christians* — that is the great thing. I can't go to your school to be your new scholar today. But I am very glad you asked me. It shows that you are zealous in a good cause, and I hope that you will ever be so as you grow up. And I do not want you to think that I am too old to go to Sunday school. No one is ever too old to study the truths of the Bible."

When he died, all the schools of Lexington were closed, and the children wept with the grown people when they heard that their kind friend was dead.

A gentleman tells this story, which is quite in keeping with General Lee's way of pleasing children:

"When my little girl, about four years old, heard of General Lee's death, she said to me, 'Father, I can never forget General Lee.' I asked, 'Why?' 'Because, when Maggie and I were playing at the gate the other day, and General Lee was riding by, he stopped and took off his hat and bowed to us and said, 'Young ladies, don't you think this is the prettiest horse you ever saw?' And we said it was a very pretty horse. 'Oh, no,' he said; 'I want to know whether Traveler is not the very prettiest horse you ever saw in your life.' And when we looked at him, and saw how white and gay he was, we said, 'Yes.' Then he laughed and said, 'Well, if you think he is so pretty, I will just let you kiss him'; and then he rode off smiling, and I don't believe I can ever forget that."

General Lee on Traveler

Another gentleman, who was clerk of the faculty at Washington College, says General Lee was very careful about little things. One day the clerk wrote a letter to some one at General Lee's request, in which he used the term "our students." When General Lee looked at it, he said that he did not like the phrase "our students." He said that we had no property rights in the young men, and he thought it best to say, "*the* students," not "*our* students." The clerk struck out with his pen the word "our" and wrote

The Life of General Robert E. Lee

"the." He then brought the letter to General Lee. "This will not answer," said he. "I want you to write the letter over." So the clerk had to make a fresh copy.

One day General Lee directed him to go to the Mess Hall and measure for a stovepipe. "Set the stove in its place on its legs," he said, "and measure the height to a point opposite the flue-hole, and then the space from the joint to the wall." The man returned with the measure. "Did you set the stove on its legs?" asked the General. The clerk replied no; that the legs were packed up inside the stove, and that he simply allowed for the legs. "But I told you to put the stove on its legs and then measure. Go back and do as you were told," said the General, who was always kind but meant to be obeyed.

The same gentleman remembers this amusing incident:

One day they saw a gentleman coming up the lawn, and wondered who he was. General Lee shook hands with him as though he knew him, and chatted for some time. He tried in vain to remember his name. In the meantime Rev. J. William Jones, whose month it was to lead the services in the chapel, came up and whispered to General Lee to introduce the strange clergyman to him, so that he might ask him to conduct the services in his place. But General Lee, with his own ready tact, said: "Mr. Jones, it is time for service; you had better go in the chapel."

After service, when he could do so without being heard, General Lee asked Mr. Jones to find out the stranger's name. He had met him in the Mexican war but could not recall his name. Mr. Jones did so, and General Lee, standing near, heard it, and then, without making it known he had forgotten his friend of the Mexican war, introduced him to those who were near. He could not think of hurting the clergyman's feelings by letting him know he had been forgotten.

General Lee was always careful not to injure what belonged to others.

"A Southern Girl" tells this story of him:

"When in Maryland, he gave strict orders that no harm should be done to property, and was once seen to get down from his horse and put up a fencerail that his men had thrown down."

This story of General Lee went the rounds of the Southern newspapers in 1864:

"On the train to Petersburg, one very cold morning, a young soldier, with his arm in a sling, was making great efforts to put on his overcoat. In the midst of his trouble, an officer rose from his seat, went to him and kindly helped him, drawing the coat gently over the wounded arm, and then with a few kind words went back to his seat.

"Now, the officer was not clad in a fine uniform with a gilt wreath on his collar and many straps on his sleeves, but he had on a plain suit of gray, with only the three gilt stars which every Confederate colonel could wear. And yet, he was no other than our chief general, Robert E. Lee, who is not braver than he is good and modest."

In the winter of 1864, some of the cavalry were moved to Charlottesville, in order to get food for their horses, and not having much to do, the officers began to attend dances. General Lee, hearing of this, wrote to his son Robert thus:

"I am afraid that Fitz was anxious to get back to the ball. This is a bad time for such things. * * There are too many Lees on the committee. I like them all to be at battles, but I can excuse them at balls."

It is said during the seven days' battle, of which I have told you, he was sitting under a tree, the shades of evening hiding even the stars on his coat collar, when a doctor rode up and said:

"Old man, I have chosen that tree for my field hospital and I want you to get out of the way."

"I will gladly give way when the wounded come up, but in the meantime there is plenty of room for both of us," was the reply.

The angry man was about to make some retort when a staff officer rode up and spoke to his "old man" as General Lee.

The doctor then began to make excuse for his rudeness, but General Lee said quietly:

"It is no matter, Doctor; there is plenty of room till your wounded come up."

This story is often told of him: In 1864, when General Lee was on the lines below Richmond, many soldiers came near him and thus brought to them the fire of the foe. He said to the soldiers: "Men, you had better go into the backyard; they are firing up here and you might get hurt."

The men obeyed, but saw their dear General walk across the yard and pick up some object and place it in a tree over his head. They found out the object he had risked his life for was only a little bird which had fallen out of its nest. God had given the stern chief a heart so tender that he could pause amid a rain of shot and shell to care for a tiny fallen birdling.

General Lee dearly loved his horses. Once, when at the springs, he wrote to his clerk in Lexington and sent this message to his horse, Traveler: "Tell him I miss him dreadfully."

Traveler lived only two years after the death of his master. In the summer of 1872, when he was fifteen years old, the fine, faithful animal, that had carried the General through the storms of war and the calm of his latter years, died of lock-jaw in Lexington. He was noted for his springy walk, high spirit, and great strength. When a colt, he was called Jeff Davis. The General changed his name to Traveler. He was his most famous war-horse.

In the summer of 1862, General Lee owned a beautiful war-horse called Richmond, given to him by some friends in the city of Richmond. But, to the grief of his master, this pet was short-lived; and what he writes after his loss, sounds almost as if he were looking back to the death of a friend:

"His labors are over, and he is at rest. He carried me very faithfully, and I shall never have so beautiful an animal again."

General Lee was noted for his want of hatred towards any one. He called the Northern soldiers "those people." Once, in the midst of a fierce battle, he said to his son Robert, who was bravely working at a big gun, "That's right, my son; drive those people back." When told of Jackson's fatal wound, his eye flashed fire and his face flushed as he thought of his great loss; but he quietly said:

"General Jackson's plans shall be carried out. Those people *shall be* driven back *today*."

The Rev. J. William Jones says — one day after the war, as he went up the street, he saw General Lee standing talking to a poor man. As the man walked away he said to him: "That is one of the old soldiers, and added, 'he fought on the other side; but we must not think of that.'"

After the war, when at the springs, a lady friend pointed to a man near by and said to General Lee, "That is General _____, of the Federal Army. He is having quite a dull time. He is here with his daughters, but we do not care to have anything to do with them."

"I am glad that you told me," said General Lee; "I will see at once that they have a better time."

After that he took pains to make friends with "those people," and so set the fashion for others. General _____ and his daughters were soon having "a better time."

General Lee was more than brave and tender; he was meek, yet with a heart big enough to love every one of his soldiers, and great enough to plan long marches and glorious battles.

After the battle of Gettysburg, one of his officers rode up and told him his men were for the most part killed or wounded. Lee shook hands with him and said: "All this has been my fault. It is *I* who have lost this fight, and you must help me out as best you can."

Not once did Lee cast the blame where it belonged, but rode among his men with such words of cheer as these: "All this will come right in the end." "We want all good and true men just now." "All good men must rally." In this way he closed up his broken lines, and showed such a brave front that Meade did not deem it well to renew the fight.

Once, when some friends were at his house in Richmond, the Rev. Dr. _____ spoke in sharp terms of the way in which the North had acted. General Lee said, "Well! it matters little what they may do to me; I am old, and have but a short time to live at best."

Pickett's Return After the Battle of Gettysburg

When Dr. _____ got up to go home, General Lee went with him to the door and said to him, "Doctor, there is a good book which I read, and which you preach from, which says, 'Love your enemies, bless them that curse you, do good to them that hate you.' Do you think your speech just now quite in that spirit?"

When Dr. _____ made some excuse, General Lee said: "I fought the people of the North because I believed that they were seeking to wrest from the South her rights. * * * I have never seen the day when I did not pray for them."

One day during the war, as they were looking at the hosts of the foe, one of his generals said, "I wish those people were all dead!" General Lee, with that grace which was his own, said, "How can you say so? Now, I wish that they would all go home and leave us to do the same."

At the close of the war, some of our best men went to seek homes in other lands. This, General Lee deemed wrong. He thought the men of the South should stay at home and build up what had been laid waste by war. He wrote to one of his friends thus: "She (Virginia) has need for all of her sons, and can ill afford to spare you." Once more he wrote: "I think the

South needs the aid of her sons more than at any time of her history. As you ask, I will state that I have no thought of leaving her."

In a word, the welfare of the impoverished, desolated South was his chief concern. He kept in sight the honor of the South, but not that hate to the North which brought no good.

A lady who had lost her husband in the war, and had brought her two sons to college, spoke in sharp terms of the North to General Lee. He gently said: "Madam, do not train up your children as foes to the Government of the United States. * * We are one country now. Bring them up to be Americans." Thus did this grand man, with a sad heart, try to do his duty at all times and on all occasions.

Though meek in the way I have told you, General Lee was at the same time too proud to take the aid which, from time to time, his friends would offer him. They knew that he had lost his "all" by the war, and felt that he should now be helped, so that he might pass his days without care. But this proud man would take no aid. When, in a quiet way, the trustees of the college gave the house in which he lived to Mrs. Lee, and also the sum of three thousand dollars each year, he wrote, in Mrs. Lee's name, a kind but firm letter and declined the gift.

After his death, they again deeded the home to Mrs. Lee and sent her a check for a large sum of money. But she, with the pride of her husband, sent back the check and would not let the funds of the college be taken for her use.

General Lee was always neat in his attire. This trait was the cause of much comment at the time of the "surrender."

General Sharp, of the Federal Army, says:

"It was late in the day when it was known that General Lee had sent for General Grant. The surrender took place in the left-hand room of an old house which had a hallway through it. In that room were a few officers, of whom I was one.

"A short space apart sat two men. The larger and taller of the two was the more striking. His hair was as white as snow. There was not a speck

upon his coat; not a spot upon those gauntlets that he wore, which were as bright and fair as a lady's glove. That was Robert E. Lee. The other was Ulysses S. Grant. His boots were muddy, and he wore no sword.

"The words which passed between Lee and Grant were few. General Grant, while the men wrote out the terms of the surrender, said: 'General Lee, I have no sword; I rode all night.' And General Lee, with the pride which became him well, made no reply, but in a cold, formal way, bowed.

"Then General Grant, in the attempt to be polite, said: 'I don't always wear a sword.'

"Lee only bowed again.

"Some one else then said: 'General Lee, what became of the white horse you rode in Mexico? He may not be dead yet; he was not so old.'

"General Lee again bowed and said: 'I left him at the White House, on the Pamunkey river, and I have not seen him since.'

"Then there were a few words, which we could not hear, spoken in a low tone of voice between Grant and Lee.

"At last, when the terms of surrender had all been signed, Lee arose, cold and proud, and bowed to each man on our side in the room. And then he went out and passed down that little square in front of the house, and mounted the gray horse that had carried him all over Virginia.

"When he had gone we learned what the low-toned words had meant. General Grant turned and said: 'You go and ask each man that has three rations to turn over two of them, and send them on to General Lee. His men are on the point of starvation.'"

This calm, proud man was the same who a few hours before had said: "Then there is nothing left me but to go and see General Grant, and I would rather die a thousand deaths." His superb, proud men won from the foe only praise and respect.

I must here give you General Fitzhugh Lee's picture of the two generals at that time:

"Grant, not yet forty-three years old, five feet eight inches tall, shoulders slightly stooped, hair and beard nut-brown, wearing a dark-blue blouse; top-boots, pants inside; dark thread gloves; without spurs or sword, and no marks of rank save the straps of a general.

"Lee, fifty-eight years old, six feet tall, hair and beard silver-gray; a handsome uniform of Confederate gray, buttoned to the throat, with three stars on collar, fine top-boots with spurs, new gauntlets, and at his side a splendid sword." Lee wore his best in honor of the cause for which he fought.

General Lee never touched tobacco, brandy or whiskey; he was always a sober man. Just as he was starting to the Mexican war, a lady in Virginia gave him a bottle of fine old whiskey, saying that he would be sure to need it, and that it was very fine. On his return home he sent the bottle, unopened, to his friend to convince her that he could get along without whiskey.

The Life of General Robert E. Lee

General Lee once proposed to treat some of his officers, saying, "I have a demijohn which I know *is of the best.*" The demijohn was brought, and the cups, held out for the treat, were filled to the brim — not with old "Rye," but with fresh buttermilk, which a kind lady had sent. The General seemed to enjoy the joke hugely.

Being once asked to a fine dinner, he refused all the good dishes, and said to the lady of the house: "I cannot consent to be feasting while my poor men are nearly starving."

It was his way to send any nice thing he might have to the sick and wounded in the hospitals.

A lady relates that when her brother was badly wounded near Petersburg, he was taken to a tent near a hospital, out of range of the fire of the foe. One day General Lee came riding up and went in to see the wounded man. He took him gently by the hand and told him to cheer up and get well; that he had use for all brave men like him. Then he drew two fine peaches from his pocket and laid them on the side of the cot.

Tears trickled down the wounded man's pale cheeks as he listened to these kind words, and felt that his chief cared so much for him, a private soldier.

Near the close of the war, when meat had become quite scarce, an aide of President Davis', being at headquarters, was asked to dine. The meal spread on the rough board was cornbread, and a small piece of meat in a large mess of greens. The aid saw the meat was not touched, though General Lee had asked all to take a piece of it. When the meal was over, the aide asked one of the men why the meat was not eaten. The reply was, that it had been loaned by a friend to cook with the greens, and had to be returned.

It was General Lee's wish to fare just as his men did. When, during the siege of Petersburg, Mrs. Lee, fearing the great strain would be too much for him begged him to take more care of his health, he wrote: "But what care can a man give to himself in time of war?" He then went on to say he lived in a tent in order to be near his men and the officers with whom he had to act; that he had been offered rooms by kind friends, but he could not turn their homes into a camp.

An English officer wrote this account of Lee's headquarters in 1862: "Lee's headquarters I found were only seven or eight pole-tents, with their backs to a stake-fence, while a little stream of good water flowed close by. In front of the tents were three wagons, and a number of horses roamed over the fields. No guards were seen near, and no crowd of aids swarmed about. A large farmhouse stood close by, which would have made a good home for the General, but Lee does not let his men rob or disturb the people, and likes to set them a good example."

It was in this way that he gained the great love of his men.

A short time after the surrender, two ragged Confederates, just from prison in the North, waited upon the General and said that there were sixty other fellows around the corner who were too ragged to come. They had sent these two to offer their loved chief a home in the mountains of Virginia. "We will give you," said one of them, "a good house and a fine farm. We boys will work for you and you shall never want."

Tears came to the eyes of General Lee as he told them that he must decline their gift. The offer of these men was but the feeling of the whole South. Though poor themselves, they would have given him houses, lands and money had he let them.

Just after the war, General Lee received the following letter from one of his old soldiers:

> "Dear General:
>
> "We have been fighting hard four years, and now the Yankees have got us in Libby Prison. They are treating us awful bad. The boys want you to get us out if you can; but if you can't, just ride by the Libby and let us see you and give you a cheer. We will all feel better for it."

Libby Prison

This letter touched the tender heart of Lee, as well as this story which was told to him by Rev. J. William Jones: After the war, the latter was riding along a road one day, when he saw a young man plowing in a field, guiding the plow with one hand, for on the other side was an empty sleeve.

He soon saw that the man plowing was a soldier whom he had known, and stopped to speak to him. In fact, he had known the young man from boyhood; how, at the first tap of the drum he had gone to fight for his native State; and how he had been maimed for life, and had gone home to find that he must work with one arm for his bread, as his fortune had been wrecked by the war. When he told the young man how sad it made him to see him thus, the latter said: "Oh! it is all right. I thank God that I have one arm left, and can use it for those I love."

When the Rev. Mr. Jones told this to General Lee, his face flushed, and he said: "What a noble fellow! But it is just like one of our soldiers. The world has never seen nobler men than those who belonged to the Army of Northern Virginia."

The real cornerstone of Lee's life was his trust in God. Whatever came to him he always said, "God's will be done."

The death of the wife of his son, General W. H. Fitzhugh Lee, gave General Lee much grief. The former General was wounded and taken prisoner. While in prison his lovely wife died. In this bitter grief, General Lee wrote to his son these words:

"My whole trust is in God, and I am ready for whatever He may ordain."

While the army was at Mine Run, in November, 1863, and a battle was at hand, General Lee, with a number of officers riding down the line of battle, came upon a party of soldiers who were holding a prayer meeting. The shooting had begun along the lines, the cannon were already roaring, and the mind and heart of the great chief were on the battle. Yet, as he saw these men bent in prayer, he dismounted and joined in the simple worship. So these humble men led the devotions of their loved General.

One day in 1865, while riding along the lines with his staff, General Lee met the Rev. J. William Jones, who was giving tracts to the men in the trenches. He at once reined in his horse and spoke to this "man of God," while the officers crowded around.

General Lee asked if he ever had calls for prayer books, and said that if he would come to his headquarters he would give him some — that a friend in Richmond had given him a new book; and upon his saying to his friend he would give his old book, he had used ever since the Mexican war, to some soldier, the friend offered him a dozen new books for the old one. He had, of course, taken so grand an offer, and now had twelve, in place of one, to give away.

When the Rev. Mr. Jones called, General Lee was out, but had left the books for Mr. Jones with one of his staff. He had written on the fly-leaf of each book, "Presented by R. E. Lee."

We are sure if any of these books were saved amid the din and stress of war, they are now much prized by those who own them.

These are some of the words which General Lee would use when his army had gained the day: "Thanks be to God." "God has again crowned the valor of our troops with success." Again, upon a fast-day, he said in an order, "Soldiers! let us humble ourselves before the Lord our God, asking, through Christ, the forgiveness of our sins."

With the close of the war, the piety of this great man seemed to increase. His seat at church was always filled, unless he was kept away by sickness, and he was ever ready for good works. He did not find fault with preachers, as so many do, but was most fond of those who were simple and true to the teachings of the Bible.

Once he said to a friend: "Do you think that it would be any harm for me to hint to Mr. _____ that we should be glad if he made his *morning prayers* a little short? You know our friend makes this prayer too long. He prays for the Jews, the Turks, and the heathen, and runs into the hour for our College recitations. Would it be wrong for me to hint to Mr. _____ that he confine his morning prayers to us *poor sinners at the College*, and pray for the Turks, the Jews, the Chinese, and other heathen some other time?"

General Lee was a constant reader of the Bible. One of his friends relates, as he watched beside his body the day after death, he picked up from the table a well-worn pocket Bible, in which was written in his own hand, "R. E. Lee, Lieutenant Colonel of U. S. Army." This little book had been the light of his pathway through many trials.

General Lee gave freely of his small means to his church and to the poor. At a vestry meeting which took place the evening of his illness, the sum of fifty-five dollars was needed for the pay of the Rector. Though he had before given his share, General Lee said in a low voice, "I will give the sum." These were the last words he spoke to the vestry, and this giving was his last public act.

His love for his wife and children is shown by the tender, loving letters he wrote when away from them. During the War Between the States ("Civil War") his anxiety for them was great.

Just before the Northern army crossed the Potomac, in 1861, Mrs. Lee left her beautiful home, Arlington, and came South. Arlington was at once seized by the Northern Government, and the grounds were taken for a burial-place for the Northern soldiers.

Mrs. Lee and her daughters then sought a home at the "White House," on the Pamunkey river, where Washington married the "Widow Custis," and

Residence of General Lee in Richmond

which had been left by Mr. Custis to one of General Lee's sons. Mrs. Lee and her daughters were soon driven from there by the hosts of McClellan, and the house was burned to the ground. At last, they found a home in Richmond, where they lived until the close of the war.

Mrs. Lee's health had failed, but a large part of her time was spent in knitting socks for the poor bare-footed soldiers of the South. Her brave daughters, also, knit socks, and nursed the sick and wounded soldiers.

Those were sad times, and the Lee family suffered most heavily.

The death of her noble husband was a great shock to Mrs. Lee, who was then not able to walk without aid. She did not survive him many years, and now rests beside him in the College chapel at Lexington, Virginia. Their daughter Agnes, who died shortly after her father, is buried in the same place.

Mary Custis Lee

Close by is the grave of Stonewall Jackson. How neat these two friends and heroes should rest so near each other!

The blue mountains of their loved Virginia keep "watch and ward" over their graves; and each year, pilgrims from every part of the land come to visit their tombs and place fresh flowers and green wreaths upon them.

The Life of General Robert E. Lee

General Custis Lee was made president of the College in his father's place. The College is now called the "Washington and Lee University," after Washington and Lee, the two great names in the history of our country.

Cŏn'cōurse, a crowd of people.
Cou'rier (kōō'rier), a man who carries an order for an officer.
Pĭl'grim, a traveler to holy places.

Tell me —
What General Lee became in 1865.
Something about his work.
His visit to the South in 1870.
His illness and death.
What day is kept throughout the South in memory of Lee?
About Mrs. Lee.
The tomb of Lee.
Washington and Lee University.

Lee's Coat of Arms

CHAPTER VII
A People's Hero

After the death of General Lee, many speeches were made in his praise, and many letters were written telling of the sorrow of his friends. These letters came not only from the South, but from the North, and other lands.

The *New York Sun* thus closes its notice:

"His death will awaken great grief through the South, and many people in the North will drop a tear of sorrow on his bier. * * * In General Lee, an able Soldier, a sincere Christian, and an honest man has been taken from earth."

The *New York Herald* said these kind words of him:

"In a quiet autumn morning, in the land he loved so well, and, as he held, he had served so faithfully, the spirit of Robert E. Lee left the clay which it had so much ennobled, and traveled out of this world into the great and unknown land. * * *

"Not to the Southern people alone shall be limited the tribute of a tear over the dead Virginian. Here in the North, forgetting that the time was when the sword of Robert E. Lee was drawn against us, we have long since ceased to look upon him as the Confederate leader, but have claimed him as one of ourselves; for Robert Edward Lee was an American, and the great nation which gave him birth would today be unworthy of such a son if she looked upon him lightly."

The *Pall Mall Gazette*, London, England, said:

"The news from America, that General Robert E. Lee is dead, will be received with great sorrow by many in this country, as well as by his fellow-soldiers in America.

"It is but a few years since Robert E. Lee ranked among the great men of his time. He was the able soldier of the Southern Confederacy, the leader

who twice threatened, by the capture of Washington, to turn the tide of success and cause a revolution which would have changed the destiny of the United States."

The *London Standard* gave this tribute to Lee:

"A country which has given birth to men like him, and those who followed him, may look the chivalry of Europe in the face without shame; for the lands of Sidney and of Bayard never brought forth a nobler soldier, gentleman and Christian, than Robert E. Lee."

He was called "the great captain of his age"—"the great general of the South"—"a good knight, noble of heart and strong of purpose, and both a soldier and a gentleman."

These beautiful words were said of him in a speech soon after his death:

"General Lee's fame is not bounded by the limits of the South, nor by the continent. I rejoice that the South gave him birth. I rejoice that the South will hold his ashes. But his fame belongs to the human race. Washington, too, was born in the South and sleeps in the South, but his fame belongs to mankind. We place the name of Lee by that of Washington. They both belong to the world.

"There is one thing more I wish to say before I take my seat. General Lee's fame ought to rest on its true foundation. He did not draw his sword in the cause of slavery — he did not seek to overthrow the Government of the United States. He drew it in the defense of constitutional liberty. That cause is not dead, but will live forever."

General W. Preston spoke of him thus:

"I knew him first when he was a captain. * * At that time, General Scott had decided upon General Lee as a man who would make his mark if he were ever called upon to do great work. He never drank, he never swore an oath, but there was never a dispute among gentlemen in which his voice was not more potent than any other; his rare calmness and dignity were above all. When the war came on, he followed his native State, Virginia. * * Scott maintained Lee was the greatest soldier in the army. * *

"I remember when Scott made use of these words: 'I tell you one thing, if I were on my death-bed, and knew that a battle was to be fought for my country, and the President were to say to me, 'Scott, who shall command?' I tell you that, with my dying breath, I would say Robert Lee. Nobody but Robert Lee! Robert Lee, and nobody but Lee!"

These extracts would not be complete without this one, bearing upon his life as a teacher:

"And it is an honor for all the colleges of the South, and for all our schools, that this pure and bright name is joined by the will of him that bore it with the cause of education. We believe that, so long as the name of Lee is cherished by Southern teachers, they will grow stronger in their work. They will be encouraged to greater efforts when they remember that Lee was one of their number, and that his great heart, that had so bravely borne the fortunes of an empire, bore also, amid its latest aspirations, the interests and hopes of the teacher."

A great public honor was paid to our hero when the bronze statue by Mercié (Mersea) was unveiled in Richmond.

Shortly after the death of General Lee, a few ladies met in a parlor in Richmond and formed a society known as the Ladies' Lee Monument Association. Their plan was to erect a monument in Richmond to the memory of the great chief, and to collect funds for this purpose from the entire South. They began at once their labor of love. Though the South was at that time very poor, the people gave gladly of their small means until the Ladies' Association had collected over fifteen thousand dollars.

Almost at the same time, another "Lee Monument Association" was formed of the old soldiers and sailors of the Confederacy, which had General Jubal A. Early for its president. The ladies of the Hollywood Memorial Association were asked to help, and they proved great workers in the cause.

I cannot tell you the many ways in which these and other societies worked to raise the money, but at last there was enough in the treasury to erect the statue.

In the meantime, General Fitzhugh Lee was made Governor of Virginia, and he at once began to take measures to bring about the erection of the monument. By his efforts a "Board of Managers" was appointed, whose work was to choose the design, the artist, and the site for the monument. The Allen lot, in the western part of the city, was at last chosen for the site, and was accepted as the gift of Mr. Otway Allen, June 18th, 1887. It was then the duty of the Board to find a sculptor worthy to execute this great work.

After many trials, the Board selected Monsieur Mercie, a Frenchman, who was both a painter and a sculptor of note. In the summer of 1887, the best photographs of General Lee, as well as one of his shoes and his uniform, were sent to the sculptor. A small spur, such as General Lee wore, was taken over to France by Miss Randolph, who was one of the Board of Managers. Monsieur Mercie told her when General Lee's shoe was sent to him, there was no one in his household, except his twelve-year-old boy, with a foot small enough to wear it.

In working out the likeness to General Lee, Monsieur Mercie had the good fortune to have Miss Mary Lee, who was then in Paris, as a critic of his work.

On the 27th of October, 1887, the cornerstone was laid with splendid rites, and on the 3rd of May, 1890, the statue reached Richmond by way of New York. It was packed in three boxes. On the 7th of May, each box was placed in a separate wagon, from which waved the flags of Virginia and the Confederacy. Then, one wagon was drawn by men of the city, one by old soldiers, and one by women and girls — the fine lady and her humble sister standing shoulder to shoulder. They went through the city, pulling the ropes amid the cheers of twenty thousand people, until they came to the spot where the statue was to stand. Such was their love for Lee! The monument in all is about sixty-one feet in height, and cost sixty-five thousand dollars. It shows the General mounted upon his warhorse, Traveler. His feet touch the stirrups lightly, after the manner of the Southern horsemen. He is clad in a plain uniform. A sash girds his waist, and the sword of a cavalry officer hangs from his side. He holds the bridle reins in his left hand, while in his right is his hat, which he grasps as if he had just taken it off to acknowledge the cheers of his men, through whose ranks we may suppose him to be passing.

The day decided upon for unveiling the statue was Friday, May 29th, 1890.

From North, South, East and West, people thronged to do honor to the great chief.

All the city was then thinking of one man — Lee, just as, twenty-five years before, all their hopes had turned to him.

On that day, the sun rose bright and the people with it. Soon, the noise of tramping feet and the tap of the drum were heard, and ere long the glitter of bayonets, the flashing of sabers and the waving of flags told that the line was forming. The streets were crowded, and rang with cheers as some noted soldier rode by or an old Confederate flag was waved.

At noon, the long line was formed on Broad street, and the parade began. Every window, doorway, and even the house-tops along the line of march, were filled with people eager to see the great parade, which stretched through the streets four miles in moving mass.

General Fitzhugh Lee, nephew of the hero, who had been one of his most daring cavalry generals during the war, and who had formerly been

Governor of Virginia, was chief marshal of the parade. Cheer after cheer arose as he rode by, wearing the slouch hat of a cavalryman. "Our Fitz," as his men loved to call him, "was himself again."

The guests rode in open carriages, and among them were Misses Mary and Mildred Lee; and General W. H. Fitzhugh Lee, wife and sons. They were followed by band after band of volunteer troops from all the Southern States, in the following order: South Carolina, North Carolina, Mississippi, Texas, Maryland, District of Columbia, Alabama, West Virginia and Virginia. Behind these marched the veterans — men who had fought in the War, and who came from all parts of the South. Brave men were there from Texas, the far-off "Lone Star State." With the veteran troops from Louisiana was "the old war-horse" Longstreet, who had led the First Corps of the Army of Northern Virginia; and at the head of the Georgia men was the tried and true Gordon. Gallant sons of Florida, Mississippi and Alabama were in line with the brave men of North and South Carolina. Veterans from Arkansas, Tennessee, Kentucky, Maryland, West Virginia and Virginia were also there to honor the memory of their leader.

Whenever and wherever these veterans were seen, they were greeted with hearty cheers. Some were clad in their old gray uniforms, faded and worn, and in many cases, full of bullet-holes. Here and there along the line could be seen the old and tattered flags of the Confederacy.

After the veterans, came the civic orders in Richmond, the students of Washington and Lee University, and the corps of cadets from the historic Virginia Military Institute.

The cross-bars and battle-flags of the Confederacy floated in the breeze by the side of the "Stars and Stripes," which meant that the people of the United States were one nation.

As the line moved along the streets decked with floating flags and gay bunting, the sound of the many feet was lost in loud and hearty cheers that arose from doors, house-tops and crowded sidewalks.

At last, the throng at the grandstand heard the roll of the drum and the nearing din of the parade, and soon the bright line swept into view. The crowd was so dense that persons on the grandstand could not be seen by those on the ground. Ringing cheers arose, not once, but time and time again, as the great men took their places on the stand, and it was as late as 3:45 o'clock P. M. when Governor McKinney stepped forward to make the opening speech.

Then there was prayer by Rev. Dr. Minnigerode, who was rector of St. Paul's church during the war, at which church General Lee worshiped when in Richmond.

When the prayer ended, the band played *Dixie*, the war-song of the South, with whose strains the old soldiers had so often been thrilled as they marched into battle. Then there was a great noise which at last wore itself away, and General Early rose and spoke a few words of cheer to the old soldiers.

The orator of the day was Colonel Archer Anderson, who pictured scene after scene in the life of General Lee with great force and clearness. Again the grand hero seemed to live and act in their midst — to lead them on to victory or to teach them how to bear defeat.

When the speaker took his seat, amid cheers, General Joseph E. Johnston arose and with two old soldiers marched to the base of the monument. Each of the soldiers carried a battle flag, tattered and torn by shot and shell. When the monument was reached, General Johnston pulled the rope, and one part of the veil fell off. Another pull brought off the rest of the veil, and the splendid statue was in plain view of the eager multitude. A score of old soldiers mounted its base and waved their old Confederate flags in loyal, eager love for their dead chief. Mighty cheers broke from the watching throng, like the wild breaking of a storm, but at last they died away.

Up there, against the blue sky, kissed by the rays of the setting sun, in the midst of his own people, was the matchless face and form of Lee.

Some wept, others shouted, but all thanked God that he had given to America such a son as Lee.

Seldom had men looked on such a scene before. At last the crowd went slowly away, leaving their hero in bronze to keep silent watch over the city he loved so well. Beneath him were the homes of his friends, and beyond, in "Hollywood" and "Oakwood," Richmond's "cities of the dead," were the graves of his fallen heroes, and far away, across and down the James, were his battlefields.

As time rolls on, statue and city will pass away. But the name and virtues of Robert E. Lee will never die, for they are written in the history of his country and in the *Book of Life*, and will live beyond the shores of Time.

Monsieur (mōsyur'), a French word for Mr.
Sincēré', honest.
Acknowledge (aknŏl'eg), to own a gift or favor.
Pōt'ent, strong, having power.
Sĭd'ney, an English patriot.
Bayard (bā'yär'), a French hero.
Pā'triot, one who loves his country.

Tell about —
 A great honor paid to Lee.
 The laying of the corner-stone.
 The monument.
 The parade.
 The unveiling.
 The undying fame of Lee.

GENERAL R. E. LEE'S
Farewell Address to His Soldiers

Headquarters Army Northern Virginia,
Appomattox C. H., April 10, 1865

General Orders No. 9

After four years of arduous service, marked by unsurpassed courage and fortitude, the Army of Northern Virginia has been compelled to yield to overwhelming numbers and resources.

I need not tell the survivors of so many hard-fought battles, who have remained steadfast to the last, that I have consented to this result from no distrust of them; but, feeling that valor and devotion could accomplish nothing that would compensate for the loss that must have attended a continuance of the contest, I determined to avoid the useless sacrifice of those whose past services have endeared them to their countrymen.

By the terms of the Agreement, Officers and men can return to their homes and remain until exchanged. You will take with you the satisfaction that proceeds from the consciousness of duty faithfully performed, and I earnestly pray that a merciful God will extend to you His blessing and protection. With an unceasing admiration of your constancy and devotion to your Country, and a grateful remembrance of your kind and generous consideration for myself, I bid you all an Affectionate Farewell.

Other publications from

Lincoln As The South Should Know Him
....O. W. Blacknall

Truth of the War Conspiracy of 1861
....H. W. Johnstone

A Story Behind Every Stone
.... Charles E. Purser

As You May Never See Us Again
.... Joel Craig and Sharlene Baker

Additional Information and Amendments to the North Carolina Troops 1861 – 1865 Volume I & II
.... Charles E. Purser

Memoir of Nathaniel Macon of North Carolina.......... Weldon N. Edwards

Sherman's Rascals..Frank B. Powell, III

A Southern View of the Invasion of the Southern States and War of 1861-65 .... Captain Samuel A. Ashe

A Confederate Catechism ....Lyon Gardiner Tyler

General Robert E. Lee .... Captain Samuel A. Ashe

General Lee and Santa Claus..Louise Clack

The Life of Nathaniel Macon ....William E. Dodd

The Land We Love — The South and It's Heritage............ Dr. Boyd Cathey

Pickett or Pettigrew? An Historical Essay..................... Captain W. R. Bond

A View of the Constitution of the United States of America
.... William Rawle

The Confederate Myth-Buster .... Walter D. Kennedy

Confederate States Military Prison at Salisbury, NC ... Dr. A. W. Mangum

Red State — Red County .... James R. Kennedy

Some Things For Which The South Did Not Fight
.... Dr. Henry Tucker Graham

The Retribution Conspiracy... Samuel W. Mitcham

Little Sermons in Socialism by Abraham Lincoln .... Burke McCarty

Roster of North Carolinians in Confederate Naval Service
.... LTC. (Retired) Sion H. Harrington, III

Words of Love .... Rev. Dr. W. Herman White

The Constitution of the Confederate States of America

The Adventure — Stolen Days .... Mark Vogl

More information available at
www.scuppernongpress.com

The Scuppernong Press
PO Box 1724
Wake Forest, NC 27588